On the Historical Novel

Del romanzo storico

ON THE HISTORICAL NOVEL

by Alessandro Manzoni

Translated, with an Introduction,

by Sandra Bermann

University of Nebraska Press   Lincoln & London

Copyright 1984 by
the University of Nebraska Press
All rights reserved
Manufactured in the United
States of America

Parts of the Introduction
have appeared previously in the
Canadian Review of Comparative
Literature / Revue canadienne
de littérature comparée 10,
no.1 (1983) and are reprinted
here by permission.

Publication of this book
has been aided by a grant
from the National Endowment
for the Humanities.

The paper in this book meets
the guidelines for permanence
and durability of the Committee
on Production Guidelines for
Book Longevity of the Council
on Library Resources.

Library of Congress Cataloging
in Publication Data

Manzoni, Alessandro, 1785-1873.
On the historical novel.
Translation of: Del romanzo
storico. Includes biblio-
graphical references and index.
1. Historical fiction. I. Title.
PN3441.M313   1984
809.3'81   83-10583
ISBN 0-8032-3084-2

For George and Sloan

CONTENTS

PREFACE

My purpose in translating Alessandro Manzoni's "Del romanzo storico" is quite simple. Manzoni's is the major nineteenth-century essay on the historical novel, and it has never, to my knowledge, appeared in English. In my translation, I have tried to present a readable version to Anglo-American students of the novel, aesthetics, and literary history, not to mention of Manzoni himself. Although translations of nineteenth-century Italian prose can sound quaint and convoluted to twentieth-century American ears, Manzoni's original rings with a vigor and irony that are as appealing now as they were over one hundred years ago, and I have tried to capture something of this complex energy. My Italian source was the text as originally published in the *Opere varie*, but later reprinted and edited by Michele Barbi and Fausto Ghisalberti, *Opere di Alessandro Manzoni*, vol. 2 (Milan: Casa del Manzoni, 1943). Manzoni's original includes a good number of footnotes, all of which I have translated, setting my own notes apart with a preliminary "[Ed.]." I also found helpful some of the commentary supplied by René Guise in his excellent French translation of the piece in the collection *Les Fiancés* (trans. Antoine François Marius Rey-Dussueil), *L'Histoire de la colonne infâme* (trans. Antoine de Latour), and *Du Roman historique* (trans. René Guise) (Paris: Delta, 1968), and refer to his contributions more than once in the notes of my own English version.

At many points in the essay, Manzoni quotes Latin and, in one case, Provençal texts in the original language. His readers, brought up on more classical fare, did not need translations. But most American readers do, and in an attempt to communicate as directly with the public today as Manzoni did with his own, I have left the original foreign-language text in the body of the work but offer an

English version in the footnotes. For my translations of Latin and Provençal, I have relied in varying degrees upon the work of earlier scholars: the W. M. Roberts edition of Titus Livy, *The History of Rome* (New York: Dutton and Company, 1912); the E. C. Wickham translation of Horace's *Art of Poetry* in *Horace for English Readers* (Oxford: Oxford University Press, 1903) and Bertoldi's Italian rendition of the Provençal, cited on pages 1058–59 of the *Opere di Alessandro Manzoni,* edited by Lanfranco Caretti (Milan: Ugo Mursia, 1962). Translations of Aristotle's prose as they appear in the Introduction as well as in *On the Historical Novel* are drawn directly from S. H. Butcher, *Aristotle's Poetics* (New York: Hill and Wang, 1961).

In the course of preparing this translation, I have become increasingly aware of the dearth of information available to the English-speaking student of Manzoni, especially to one interested in Manzoni's literary theory and aesthetics. Through the ample Introduction, I have tried to give some idea of Manzoni's intellectual development. But above all, I have sought to suggest to my readers the significance of *On the Historical Novel* in the larger context of literary history. For, in fact, it illuminates much more than Manzoni's own creative practice. It advances an important theory of the historical novel that deserves to be considered in itself and as it relates to other theories of the novel both before and since.

In my efforts to come to terms with the larger context of concerns Manzoni raises, I have benefited enormously from the inspiration and advice of Joseph Frank and from the incisive comments offered by Olga Ragusa on the finished manuscript. The translation itself gained much from careful readings by Robert Hollander and, especially, from the many specific suggestions of Robert Fagles. To these colleagues and the many others who listened and advised, I owe my sincerest thanks. To my husband, George, who read the entire manuscript more than once, and offered me invaluable criticism at every turn, I owe the greatest debt of all. Of course, any misjudgments in the translation or Introduction remain my own responsibility.

INTRODUCTION

Alessandro Manzoni is known today for his panoramic historical novel of seventeenth-century Italy, *I promessi sposi*. Published first in 1827, this was the crowning achievement of Manzoni's literary career and was immediately praised by an admiring public, eager for further proofs from the author they claimed as their own Sir Walter Scott. But to Manzoni, fame meant little, especially when compared with his lifelong commitment to intellectual and moral truth. In 1828, as *I promessi sposi* was rapidly coming off the press, and with linguistic revisions that would take him more than a decade already underway, Manzoni also began to write *On the Historical Novel*, an examination and eventual rejection of the historical novel as a genre. Paradoxical as it may seem, this sequence of literary events follows quite naturally from the complex forces at work within early nineteenth-century European criticism and from Manzoni's own particular set of concerns.

Manzoni lived from 1785 to 1873. He was born four years before the French Revolution and lived long enough to see, and in many ways to nurture, the political and intellectual fruits of the Italian Risorgimento. That his eighty-eight years coincide with the period associated with European Romanticism is doubtless significant, but his literary career does not permit any correspondingly neat characterization. If its source lay in late eighteenth-century neoclassical literary practice, its course was to follow the mainstream of nineteenth-century Romanticism, only to flow in the end into a larger body of thought that, for reasons to come, may be seen as a "classical" version of Romanticism. Though he left no literary school as such, and never fancied himself doing so, Manzoni left more than a great novel. His critical essays helped lay down the premises of Italian Romanticism and ultimately redefined the ongoing problematic of history's relationship to literature.

For the purposes of analysis, Manzoni's writings can conveniently be divided into three periods corresponding to distinct phases of his intellectual development. From 1801 to 1809, he wrote chiefly poetry that may be described as neoclassical in vein. Although the political and ethical themes of his early poetry would continue to occupy him in the later phases of his career, it was his adherence to prescribed eighteenth-century forms and diction that marked his work at this stage. The second and most productive of Manzoni's literary periods, stretching from 1810 to about 1827, was his years of open adherence to Romanticism. It yielded, above all, five religious poems, the *Inni sacri* (1812–22); two historical tragedies, *Il conte di Carmagnola* (1820) and the *Adelchi* (1822); an ode on the death of Napoleon, *Il cinque maggio* (1821); and finally the first edition of *I promessi sposi* (1827). This was also the time he wrote his early theoretical and historical essays—the *Osservazioni sulla morale cattolica* (1819), the Preface to *Il conte di Carmagnola* (1820), the *Discorso sopra alcuni punti della storia longobardica in Italia* (1822), the *Lettre à M. Chauvet* (1820–23), and the letter to Cesare d'Azeglio, *Sul romanticismo* (1823). Taken together, these provide Manzoni's most coherent statement on the nature of Italian Romanticism.

With his linguistic revisions of *I promessi sposi* in 1827 began a final period, during which Manzoni effectively abandoned the active writing of literature in favor of literary theory and nonfiction. What led him so preemptively to theory was a growing insistence on "truth," as he defined it, fueled by the concerted study of linguistics, history, and philosophy. It elicited from him a range of essays that might be classified as historical (*Storia della colonna infame* [1840–42] and *La rivoluzione francese del 1789 e la rivoluzione italiana del 1859* [published posthumously]), linguistic (*Sulla lingua italiana* [1846], *Intorno al libro "De vulgario eloquio" di Dante* [1868], *Intorno al vocabolario* [1868], *Dell'unitá della lingua e dei mezzi di diffonderla* (1868), and *Sentir messa* and *Della lingua italiana* [both published posthumously]), and philosophical (*Del sistema che fonda la morale sull'utilitá* [1845] and *Dell'invenzione* [1850]). But Manzoni's versatility and breadth of knowledge reveal themselves in more than the range of his writings. They also surface in his complex and probing analysis of single problems. Such is the case of his great but much neglected critical legacy, *On the Historical Novel*.

On the Historical Novel, which occupied Manzoni from 1828 to as late as 1850, effectively telescopes the author's overall intellectual development.[1] Like all Manzoni's other writings, it grew out of a rich field of literary and philosophic knowledge. But in the work, he was determined to bring all this to bear on the single, but for him profound, question of the relationship between history, on the one hand, and poetry, or (as Manzoni would name it) invention, on the other.

The Formative Years

Alessandro Manzoni was born into an intellectual and political-minded Milanese family.[2] His mother, Giulia Beccaria, was the daughter of the famous Italian jurist and criminologist Cesare Beccaria, and his legal (though probably not his natural) father was Count Pietro Manzoni, a conservative member of the lesser nobility. In spite of the many advantages offered by his family's prominence in Milanese society, the domestic setting was anything but happy, and the earliest years of Manzoni's childhood were troubled by the dissension of parents who would separate permanently in 1792.

Presumably to spare him involvement in the unhappiness, Man-

---

[1] The "Del romanzo storico e, in genere, de' componimenti misti di storia e d'invenzione," as the essay is called in the original, was first published in Manzoni's *Opere varie*. Although publication of the *Opere varie* began in 1845, the essay did not appear until 1850, when it was published along with the *Dell'invenzione* in the 6th fascicle.

[2] For additional biographical details, see S. B. Chandler, *Alessandro Manzoni* (Edinburgh: Edinburgh University Press, 1974); Archibald Colquhoun, *Manzoni and His Times* (London: J. M. Dent & Sons, 1954); Alfredo Galletti, *Alessandro Manzoni* (Milan: A. Corticelli, 1944); Attilio Momigliano, *Alessandro Manzoni* (Messina: Principato, 1929); Natalino Sapegno, *Disegno storico della letteratura italiana* (Florence: La Nuova Italia, 1966), 599–633.

zoni's parents sent him while still very young to a series of religious boarding schools—in Merate, Lugano, Magente, and Milan. Traditional in their teachings, the schools provided the child with a strong background in the standard Lombard curriculum: first and foremost, Catholic moral thought; then rhetoric, grammar, history, and a sort of philosophy, joining traditional scholasticism with the least controversial aspects of eighteenth-century rationalist and sensationalist thought. Perhaps with good reason, Manzoni found his lessons exasperatingly dull and the boarding school life little more than an intellectual prison. His only comfort, indeed his only window to intellectual excitement, was his unauthorized reading of the great eighteenth-century skeptics, particularly Voltaire and the Encyclopedists. By the time Manzoni left boarding school in 1801 to return to his father's home in Milan, his views had taken on the cast of the philosophes he had come to admire; he was anticlerical and deist in religion, sensationalist in philosophy, and neoclassical in his poetic preferences.

Once free in Milan to pursue his true intellectual interests, Manzoni gravitated to Vincenzo Monti, the most important poet of the day and a person with whom he could discuss his literary ambitions. At the same time, his early republican beliefs became stronger as he read attentively Giuseppe Parini, the great eighteenth-century poet and critic of the aristocracy, and Vittorio Alfieri, who was writing eloquently against tyranny and absolute government of any kind well up to the end of the century. During these early Milanese years, the revolutionary historian Vincenzo Cuoco urged Manzoni to study history and, in particular, Giambattista Vico's *Scienza nuova*. Readings and contacts such as these produced in Manzoni the strong humanitarian ideals and historical sensitivity that would characterize his future literary and critical achievements. Literature would always be for him, as for the poets whom as a youth he most admired, a mode of teaching; and it would serve to awaken its readers, above all, to concrete historical, political, and ethical needs. But at this point in Manzoni's intellectual development, neither the living example of Monti nor the reading of Parini or Alfieri or even Vico could singly, or in combination, organize his aesthetic standards. Many years would in fact pass before Manzoni could fully accommodate these Italian beginnings. And the moment would come only after experiences that took him well beyond his Italian home.

In 1805, the twenty-year-old was invited to Paris to live with his mother and her lover, the Milanese banker Carlo Imbonati. Imbonati died shortly before Manzoni's arrival, but the youth stayed on in Paris for the next five years. There he met the most prominent philosophers, literati, and historians of the day, several of whom—above all the young historian and man of letters, Claude Fauriel—would exert a lifelong influence upon him.[3]

Paris in the years of the Empire, between 1805 and 1810, was not yet the Paris associated with Romanticism, but neither was it in the grip of Enlightenment philosophy or of the Cartesian rationalism that had produced the scientific, philosophical, and artistic achievements of the preceding century. If anything, it was a society in the process of cultural transformation, where no single line of thought yet had the upper hand.[4]

The epigones of Descartes continued to run schools and literary salons that would sustain a belief both in nature as a rational order and in mathematical description, reason's most perfect analytic tool. They even brought to the qualitative studies of history, philosophy, and art a sort of mathematical precision through the use of sophisticated methods of analysis, elaborate categorizations, and, above all, a language whose worth was often judged by its power to efface itself before the object or idea it conveyed. Language would be transparent, clear, precise. It would communicate. Reason, with its refined instruments of human discourse, was to reveal the world and man's relationship to it. It was just as naturally taken to be the arbiter of art. Rules, unities, and genres, apparently deriving from Greek and Roman tradition but valued chiefly because they agreed with "right reason," would help guide the poet toward a beautiful and true representation of nature, one faithful to classical purposes: to teach and to please.

However much alive, the traditional classical centers did not

[3] The relationship of Manzoni's thought to that of Augustin Thierry and Fauriel is explored by Cesare De Lollis in *Alessandro Manzoni e gli storici liberali francesi della Restaurazione* (Bari: Laterza e figli, 1926).

[4] See Gustave Lanson, *Histoire de la littérature française* (Paris: Hachette, 1909), especially pt. 6, bk. 2, "L'epoque romantique"; also Francois Picavet, *Les*

attract the young Manzoni. His readings inclined him rather to the more empirical, religiously skeptical, and, at this point in French literary history, more progressive tendencies that, while emanating originally from England, had by 1805 become fully integrated into French thought. Particularly in the salon of Mme de Condorcet, where Manzoni spent some of his Parisian afternoons, he met the group of philosophers known as the *Idéologues,* led by Destutt de Tracy and Pierre-Jean-Georges Cabanis.[5] The sensationalist belief that discussion of the abstract human spirit could never lead to concrete knowledge had profound implications for the things that mattered most to Manzoni: ethics, politics, and, above all, art. How could rules of art be more than arbitrary impositions when each thing or being is but a series of sensations and, even then, sensations only as perceived by a particular mind?

The sensationalist orientation of the *Idéologues* coupled with their international interests and reformist politics, made them a natural bridge between the Enlightenment and nineteenth-century French Romantic thought. Not by accident, it was the same group, gathered at the salon of Mme de Condorcet, that came to Mme de Staël's support in her opposition to Napoleon. And there, Fauriel (who was then Mme de Condorcet's lover), a host of brilliant thinkers and historians, and Manzoni's own mother, Donna Giulia, would frequently join to discuss the political and philosophical questions of the day.

Considering Manzoni's past, it is not hard to imagine the attraction he felt for a revolutionary circle so congenial to his own political and philosophical disposition at that time. Still, if we look to Manzoni's writings for evidence of its immediate impact, we find precious little. In fact, the first fruits of this experience seem to be little more than a strengthened love for French language and literature and for the budding historical sciences, as well as a general conviction shared by the Romantics that the best poetry was a po-

---

Idéologues: Essai sur l'histoire des idées et des théories scientifiques, philosophiques, réligieuses, etc. en France depuis 1789 (Paris: Felix Alcan, 1891).

[5] The best study of Manzoni's experience with the *Idéologues* is by Elena Gabbuti, *Manzoni e gli Idéologi francesi* (Florence: Sansoni, 1936).

etry "drawn from the bottom of the heart."[6] But how would this poetry be accomplished? What would be its themes and its forms? The question marks would remain until Manzoni's life had become reorganized by a powerful ethical commitment. The impetus came within this same five-year period in the form of his conversion, or rather reconversion, to Roman Catholicism.

To this day, it is difficult to say how and why Manzoni turned back to the church whose teachings he had shrugged off in Milan. It may have reflected the gentle companionship of the young woman, Henriette ("Enrichetta") Blondel, whom he married in 1808, or simply have been the natural outcome of a long intellectual preparation that began with his early religious training and developed through his reading of Pascal and studies with the Jansenist Eustachio Dègola. It may be that, as legend has it, the conversion came at a single divine moment in the Church of Saint Roch. Perhaps it was the slowly ripening fruit of early ethical concerns. These are things we shall never know. Manzoni was deliberately reticent both in his correspondence and reported conversations about his decisive religious experience.[7] But his subsequent literary and critical works leave little doubt that his conversion to Catholicism was the emotional and rational basis for literally all his future writing. In the short run, it led him to part ways with the *Idéologues*—sensationalism, skepticism, and all—and to seek out the Romantic writers whose idealism better comported in its philosophic and artistic qualities with his own Christian fervor.

Still, Manzoni's religious change of heart was such that it produced more a change in emphasis than a complete about-face. The critic Rocco Montano goes so far as to define Manzoni's Christianity as Thomist, underscoring in this way the poet's lifelong commitment to reason and logic in the service of Christian belief.[8] Manzoni himself professed to "believe . . . with Saint Anselm and Saint

[6] Manzoni to Fauriel, Brusuglio, 20 April 1812, in *Epistolario di Alessandro Manzoni,* ed. Giovanni Sforza (Milan: Paolo Carrara, 1882), 1:124.

[7] See Chandler, *Alessandro Manzoni,* 19.

[8] Rocco Montano, *Manzoni o del lieto fine* (Naples: Conte, 1950), 109–15. For a fuller consideration of Manzoni's religious views, see Francesco Ruffini, *La vita religiosa di Alessandro Manzoni* (Bari: Laterza, 1931).

Thomas that God gave man intelligence so that he would use it not only to honor his Creator but also to correct his wayward feelings."[9] Thus, while Manzoni would align himself as a Christian with the Romantics, he would hardly be a Christian Romantic like so many others. His act of conversion was no giddy leap of faith as might have been said of Chateaubriand's. Traceable or not to his scholastic upbringing, Manzoni's evident aversion to what he felt to be the irrational or purely emotional contributed to the distance that would separate him from many who identified themselves with the Romantic movement.

From all this emerges the picture of a man attracted to, but ultimately disenchanted with, virtually every recognized school of thought he knew. The very most one could say of Manzoni as he departed Paris in 1810 was that he held certain ideas that, while still inchoate, clearly inclined him to a religious Romantic with a rational bent of mind. But perhaps more important than any conceptual framework that he may have acquired was an extraordinary inquisitiveness and an urge to write literary works in which history was a generative force. The former was part of his character, the latter a deliberate choice. A historical orientation would, he believed, respond to what he thought to be the necessities of his age and, at the same time, produce a more concrete and a more disciplined Christian poetry.

The Making of an Italian Romantic

It would probably be fair to describe Manzoni's initial views on the prospects of combining history and poetry as energetically optimistic. But then his optimism took root in particularly congenial soil. Manzoni wrote his greatest works precisely in the early years of the Risorgimento, as Italians searched for a national identity to which they expected history and historical subjects could contribute. Years earlier, writers and historiographers of postrevo-

---

[9] Alessandro Manzoni, *Osservazioni sulla morale cattolica*, quoted by Galletti, *Alessandro Manzoni*, 198.

lutionary France proceeded on the assumption that a knowledge of history would provide a sense of identity among the French people. The prospects of such knowledge contributing to a political mobilization seemed no less good in Milan in the 1820s. When Manzoni read Italian literature of that period, and especially the journal of the Italian Romantic movement, *Il conciliatore*, he was doubtless struck by the strong political mandate of the Risorgimento and its call for history. But Manzoni was hardly just a literary instrument of the movement; as his correspondence and poetry of this period amply demonstrate, he fully shared its goal of a free and united Italy.[10] That goal would be one of the central forces behind his work and his life.

Equally important, Manzoni believed that historical subjects could replace the abstract and by now stultifying classical unities with something more particularized, more real, and therefore more apt to engage his readers. Italian writers of the nineteenth century were notoriously tradition-bound compared to their contemporaries in neighboring national literatures. Had Mme de Staël not challenged the Italians to stop rehearsing stale literary formulas and to let in fresh air from abroad, the Italian debate between the classicists and Romantics might never have taken place.[11] Although Manzoni initially aligned himself in this debate with the Romantics, his distaste for literary polemics kept him from contributing to *Il conciliatore*. He did not even publish his letter *Sul romanticismo* until after the Romantics had virtually won.[12] It was above all through his creative work and, in the early twenties, particularly through his innovative historical dramas that he took his most effective stand against the falsifying strictures of the classical unities and in favor of historical subjects.

From the start, Manzoni's attachment to the Romantic movement was strongly slanted toward history, that is, toward an "objective" art, approximating life, in close communication with its pres-

---

[10] See especially the choruses of the tragedies and the lyrical ode *Marzo, 1821,* in Manzoni, *Opere varie,* ed. Michele Barbi and Fausto Ghisalberti (Milan: Casa del Manzoni, 1943).

[11] Sapegno, *Disegno,* 556.

[12] Chandler notes some differences between the original letter and the revised, published version, in *Alessandro Manzoni, 73.*

ent while focusing upon its past. In this, he stands at opposite poles from many of his contemporaries and, above all, from Leopardi, for instance, who was developing an altogether different facet of that complex movement called Romanticism—the lyric, auto-biographical, subjective—and one markedly more in line with the major strain of European Romanticism as it was being shaped by Friedrich Hölderlin, Byron, Shelley, and Alfred de Vigny. But Manzoni's more realistic and communicative vision comported better with the spirit of Italy in the 1820s, and it eventually came to be accepted as practically the defining characteristic of Italian Romanticism.[13]

This is not to suggest that Manzoni's view of Romanticism was somehow original or that he claimed it to be. It was more the product of a deliberate literary and philosophical eclecticism:

> Some writers, fed up with the pedantry and falseness that prevail in received theories of poetry and literature in general, struck by the truths about the doctrine of the beautiful scattered in some French, German, English, and Italian writings, have paid particular attention to these questions. Without adopting any of the various solutions proposed by the philosophical men of letters, they gathered on all sides what seemed true to them; they put to one side those that resulted from local conditions and particular philosophical systems, or even national prejudices; and they rallied round a general principle that they expounded, that they enriched with new evidence, and that they elevated, it seems to me, in leaving to it and its doctrines the name Romanticism, even though the name does not represent for them the same group of ideas to which it referred in other nations.[14]

Manzoni's methodology demanded a current acquaintance with literary and philosophical developments abroad. As it was, he had kept pace, even after his return to Milan, thanks largely to the letters and books sent to him by his Parisian friend Fauriel.[15] By

---

[13] Mario Puppo, *Poetica e critica del romanticismo* (Milan: Marzorati, 1973), 62–90.

[14] Manzoni, *Lettre à M. Chauvet*, in *Opere varie*, 365.

[15] See Joseph Francis De Simone, *Alessandro Manzoni: Esthetics and Literary*

any standard, but certainly by that of an Italian of the time, the library that Manzoni had accumulated was both current and cosmopolitan. A handful of writers, however, stood out as his most important artistic and critical models.

Two of them—Shakespeare and Walter Scott—were English. It was not that Manzoni was an anglophile, for the mainstays of English Romanticism, chiefly the lyric poets, held little for him. Shakespeare, however, epitomized for Manzoni, as for many of the Romantics, a genial use of organic form; Manzoni would make this clear in several of his essays, including *On the Historical Novel*.[16] The unities were of no concern to Shakespeare, who seemed to find the rules of art inscribed rather in each individual subject. More important, a good many of his subjects had a Christian orientation and a historical basis. For this reason, they were not what Manzoni would call "arbitrary," a term he reserved in his early years for subjects lacking any grounding in objective truth.[17] In any case, the subjects that Shakespeare chose enabled him to produce what seemed to Manzoni the greatest dramas of all time.

Walter Scott's appeal was different, not because he was so much in vogue, though in fact he was, but because his literary use of history was groundbreaking. For Manzoni, as for Georg Lukács a century later, Scott was the "Homer of the historical novel," discoverer of the "derivation of the individuality of characters from the historical peculiarities of their age."[18] Still, if Scott used history more effectively than previous novelists, his historical sense was not, Manzoni would say, as keen or profound as it should have been. As early as 1821, Manzoni writes:

Criticism (New York: Vanni, 1946), for a description of Manzoni's attitudes toward his foreign contemporaries, and on Fauriel, pp. 367–70.

[16] The *Lettre à M. Chauvet* includes an analysis of *Richard II*, and comments on Shakespeare also appear in the preface to *Il conte di Carmagnola*. Manzoni praises Shakespeare in *On the Historical Novel*, Part II. No doubt Shakespeare gained in stature for Manzoni at least in part because of the central place he held in the minds of the German Romantics with whom Manzoni was familiar.

[17] See especially the *Lettre à M. Chauvet*, 313–71; and the *Lettre à Victor Cousin*, in *Tutte la opere di Alessandro Manzoni*, ed. A. Chiari and Fausto Ghisalberti, vol. 3 (Milan: Mondadori, 1962), 581–639.

[18] Georg Lukács, *The Historical Novel*, trans. Hannah and Stanley Mitchell (Lincoln: University of Nebraska Press, 1983), 19; 19–63.

I conceive historical novels as portraying a given state of society through facts and characters so similar to reality that one might think one has just come upon a veritable history. When historical events and characters are introduced, they should be portrayed in the most strictly historical of ways. So, for instance, Richard the Lion-Hearted seems defective to me in *Ivanhoe.*[19]

That Manzoni was a more meticulous historian, not to mention a more meticulous author, than Walter Scott is evident from comparing *I promessi sposi* with virtually any of Scott's novels. But, then, his purpose was altogether different. If Scott intended his novel, to use his own words, to be "a mere elegance, a luxury contrived for the amusement of polished life and the gratification of that half-love of literature which pervades all ranks in an advanced state of society," Manzoni wrote to convey "the true, the useful, the good, the rational."[20]

Like Scott, Manzoni was drawn to the works of Goethe, though unlike Scott, he was drawn to only one phase of them. He was predictably uninterested in *Werther, Wilhelm Meister,* or even *Faust,* each too clearly a creature of the author's imagining. It is with Goethe's historical dramas in mind that Manzoni would call him, in *On the Historical Novel,* the one modern playwright willing to follow in Shakespeare's footsteps.

In fact, Manzoni took much more from Germany than a third literary model. He drew on all that the developments in German historiography and philosophy might contribute to his own understanding of art, insisting, however, that it be in fundamental harmony with his own ideas. An affinity to his own rational religiosity, for example, reconciles Manzoni's quick responsiveness to Kant and some of the early German Romantics with his rejection of their followers, at least to the extent that they injected an arbitrariness or subjectivity he found alien.[21] He doubtless gleaned from them some

[19] Manzoni, *Epistolario* 1:214.

[20] Sir Walter Scott, *Lives of the Novelists* (London: Oxford University Press, 1906), 21. Manzoni's aims are expressed indirectly in *Sul romanticismo,* in *Opere varie,* 619.

[21] See especially Manzoni's *Lettre à Victor Cousin,* 581–639 for his views on nineteenth-century philosophy.

general awareness of the subject-object problematic that dominated so much of German thought at that time and a more specific insight into the novel's relationship to the epic. Among the early Romantic theorists, August Wilhelm Schlegel exerted a special attraction for Manzoni, at least in part because he strongly linked Romanticism with Christianity and struck the importance of organic form:

> Form is mechanical when, through external force, it is imparted to any material merely as an accidental addition without reference to its quality. . . . Organic form, again, is innate; it unfolds itself from within and acquires its determination contemporaneously with the perfect development of the germ. . . . In the fine arts, as well as in the domain of nature—the supreme artist—all genuine forms are organic, that is, determined by the quality of the work. In a word, the form is nothing but a significant exterior, the speaking physiognomy of each thing which, as long as it is not disfigured by any destructive accident, gives a true evidence of its hidden essence.[22]

To the most important figures of the French Romantic movement, Manzoni showed indifference, if not aversion. Chateaubriand's emotional embrace of Christianity he found inauthentic, and Victor Hugo's talent robust but disoriented. Of Stendhal he says nothing at all. Only Mme de Staël, whose *De l'Allemagne* and *De la littérature* helped introduce him to Romanticism, and the poet Lamartine, whom he seems to have admired more for his liberal politics than his poetry, won mild praise.[23]

The French authors Manzoni most prized were not literary figures at all, but scholars and chiefly historians. Guizot and Augustin Thierry would lead him, some time after his return from Paris, to the new French historiography, a school of historical science for which dynasties and battles were distinctly not enough.[24] These early Romantic historians, not unlike Voltaire some seventy-five years before, made customs, art, and literature their field. But un-

[22] August Wilhelm Schlegel, *Course of Lectures on Dramatic Art and Literature,* trans. John Black (London: Henry G. Bohn, 1846), 340.

[23] De Simone, *Alessandro Manzoni: Esthetics,* 342–54.

[24] See Emery Neff, *The Poetry of History* (New York: Columbia University Press, 1947), 116–28.

like their predecessors, they made the oppressed masses their focus. Equally important, they considered literary art to be a necessary ingredient in the writing of history itself. Thierry, for instance, directly attributed his vocation as a historiographer to the literary inspiration of Chateaubriand's *Les martyrs* and his distinct concrete narrative style to his reading of Walter Scott's *Ivanhoe:*

> Walter Scott had cast one of his eagle glances upon the historical period toward which all the effort of my thought had been directed for three years. With characteristic boldness he had placed on English soil Normans and Saxons, victors and vanquished, still quivering with resentment in each other's presence one hundred and twenty years after the conquest. He had colored poetically one long scene of the long drama I was laboring to construct with the patience of a historian.[25]

From this moment, Thierry attempted to produce "art at the same time as science." He developed what would be known as narrative history, a historical style that attested to the real, that made it believable by incorporating as many details, as many "facts," as possible. Such a narrative technique would be for Manzoni, too, the method by which good history was made.[26]

Manzoni's choice of literary models, like his choice of subject matter and technique, reveals at every turn the close connection he wished to forge between history and the highest forms of art. But to identify an appreciation for historical poetry as peculiar to Manzoni's Italian Romanticism is not to suggest that others, long before the modern Romantic period, had not carefully weighed the joining of history and poetry. They had, and quite critically. The problematic of the relationship between history and poetry has venerable origins; and while Manzoni did not systematically trace them in any of his essays—as he traced the genesis of the historical novel as such—his occasional references to ancient, Renaissance, and nineteenth-century criticism show that he was aware of them.

---

[25] Augustin Thierry, *Dix ans d'études historiques* (Paris: Furne, Jouvet, n.d.), 9.
[26] Thierry, *Dix ans,* 13. For Manzoni's comments on historical narrative, see Part I of *On the Historical Novel.*

The Critical Tradition

It was Aristotle who in the fourth century B.C. compared history to poetry from a perspective that clearly favored poetry:

> The poet and the historian differ not by writing in verse or in prose. The work of Herodotus might be put into verse, and it would still be a species of history, with meter no less than without it. The true difference is that one relates what has happened, the other what may happen. . . . Poetry, therefore, is a more philosophical and a higher thing than history, for poetry tends to express the universal, history the particular. By the universal I mean how a person of a certain type will on occasion speak or act, according to the law of probability or necessity.[27]

Manzoni knew Aristotle's preference well; there is one reference or another to him in each of Manzoni's critical essays, and the above passage appears in a long footnote to *On the Historical Novel*. But he also knew that by the 1820s poetry's advantage over history as a vehicle for conveying universal truth had become far less pronounced. The dichotomy itself was called into question by at least two intervening developments: the evolution of a philosophy of history and the recognition that historical and fictional writing might rest on certain common rhetorical principles.[28]

If Aristotle denied history a universal character and, therefore, the stature of poetry or philosophy, it was largely because Greek antiquity did not produce the sort of systematic philosophies of history characteristic of later centuries.[29] His exclusion of rhetoric was more intentional. Aristotle, like Plato before him, consciously subordinated the question of rhetoric to the more important study of

---

[27] Aristotle, *Poetics,* trans. S. H. Butcher (New York: Hill and Wang, 1961), 68.

[28] Nancy S. Streuver presents an excellent discussion of the dependence of history upon rhetoric in *The Language of History in the Renaissance* (Princeton, N.J.: Princeton University Press, 1970).

[29] One might, of course, argue that Thucydides and, to some extent, Herodotus gave us the first philosophies of history. It is only when compared to later historical texts, those that would develop after Augustine, and particularly in the nineteenth century, that their philosophical nature pales.

logic and truth.[30] Bracketing the matter of rhetoric made categorization and the apparent attainment of truth easier. But then rhetoric is never a welcome question for metaphysicians. It inevitably places a premium on coherence, unity, and form, qualities that attenuate the strict correspondence of language to concrete or even metaphysical reality; it may confuse or, worse yet, pervert.

Not until Cicero, who described history as a particularly demanding *opus oratorium*, were the rhetorical implications of historical writing genuinely recognized.[31] It was among Cicero's missions to establish for rhetoric—now enlarged to encompass history and even philosophy—the status that Aristotle denied it. But the aptitude of history for conveying what is universal would not be fully realized until Augustine in his *De civitate Dei* first positioned the particulars of history within a Christian providential scheme. Once rhetoric was accepted as an art affecting all writing, and history could claim as much as poetry to be a locus of universal truth, the stage was set for the active assimilation—its critics inevitably would say confusion—of history and poetry from the Renaissance to Manzoni's own day.

History, according to Renaissance theorists like Petrarch, Coluccio Salutati, and Poggio Bracciolini, was largely the documentation of God's greater plan, as it had been for the medieval writers who preceded them. What the Renaissance humanists injected, however, were new attitudes toward the phenomenal world, marked by a pronounced interest in human action and new respect for the effective use of language.[32] Beginning particularly with Petrarch, they took up Cicero's rhetorical ideals with a vengeance. The study of eloquence, hemmed in for centuries past by logic and later by theology, now claimed priority. History, poetry, and philosophy, far from absorbing rhetoric, were themselves practically absorbed by

[30] See Streuver, *The Language of History;* also Marcia L. Colish, *The Mirror of Language,* rev. ed., (Lincoln: University of Nebraska Press, 1983); and Jerrold Seigel, "Rhetoric and Philosophy in Renaissance Humanism from Petrarch to Valla" (Ph.D. diss., Princeton University, 1963), for a discussion of classical as well as Renaissance views. The classical texts in question include Plato's *Gorgias* and *Phaedrus* and Aristotle's *Rhetoric.*

[31] Cicero *De legibus* 1.2.5. See Loeb Classical Library edition with translation by Clinton Waller Keyes (New York: G. P. Putnam's Sons, 1928).

[32] Streuver, *The Language of History,* esp. 90–100.

it; eloquent discourse became the greatest testimonial to the human mind.[33]

New respect for language brought changes in historical writing that were destined to drive it still nearer to Aristotle's concept of poetry. The demand of rhetoric for coherence, unity, and form—in a word, decorum—created a bias within the writing of history away from the accumulation of descriptive detail and toward the discovery of unifying principles. More than ever before, history sorted and construed its documents, generalized from them, even manipulated them in order to please and persuade. A certain relaxation of the ties between language and its referent was inevitable.

The sort of changes just described could not occur without dramatically emphasizing the social dimension of historical writing. That alone would not be troubling, if it did not also jeopardize its identity. But once defined primarily in rhetorical terms—as a communicative event linking author to audience—writing becomes history or poetry largely according to the author's intention and the audience's belief; and what marks history is, not its external features, which may be indistinguishable from poetry's, but the fact that it is intended and accepted as truth. Its identity has become, in a word, contingent not only on the idiosyncracies of the audience but on authorial intentions, which may as easily be to deceive as to instruct.

To be sure, the analysis that was taking shape in the fourteenth, fifteenth, and sixteenth centuries of the complex and ethically problematic marriage of history and poetry did not take quite this modern a form. But the Aristotelian commentaries of Lodovico Castelvetro and Torquato Tasso, two literary theorists to whom Manzoni will refer in his own critical essays, at least went so far as to place history and poetry on the same ontological plane unmarked by a well-defined frontier.[34] In so doing, they gave Aristotle's categories, and the hierarchy between them, their most direct critical challenge up to that time. If Castelvetro seems to favor his-

---

[33] Baldassare Castiglione's *Il cortegiano* is doubtless one of the best known Renaissance paeans to eloquence, an essential ingredient of *humanitas*.

[34] Manzoni's attitude toward the criticism of both authors is, for the most part, negative. He is particularly trenchant in criticising Castelvetro in *On the Historical Novel*, Part II, n. 78.

tory, it is probably because of his Counter-Reformation belief in history's providential pattern. "Poetry," he would say, "draws its light entirely from the light of history," and for that reason alone is practically "history's resemblance or similitude." [35] But overall, the commentary strikes such a strong rhetorical emphasis as to leave the impression that mimesis exists not so much to make a poem resemble history as simply to win the belief of the audience. Tasso, on the other hand, would distinguish history and poetry this way: history relates events, while poetry makes them come alive. But neither is relieved of having to seek truth; the one must be as firmly anchored in truth as the other, and each as firmly as any other serious genre. Just what is this truth? At one point Tasso identifies it with the historically verifiable, at another with whatever the audience takes to be true. [36] Truth thus teeters precariously between a correspondence to the real and a coherence that merely convinces.

The late Renaissance views of Castelvetro and Tasso raised ethical and intellectual perplexities that would only increase with age. By the time Manzoni himself explored them in a series of essays culminating in *On the Historical Novel*, historiography had acquired several full-fledged philosophies of history, and the rhetorical demand for decorum had found an unsuspecting successor in the nineteenth-century doctrine of the creative subject, the artistic imagination.

Philosophers of history like Jacques Bénigne Bossuet, Johann Gottfried von Herder, and Giambattista Vico clearly introduced new elements into the equation. As to these Manzoni was predictably eclectic. [37] He appreciated Bossuet's emphasis on the power of divine Providence, but regretted the meager part that the "illustrious man" seemed to leave for individual free will. For this, Herder's *Ideen zür Philosophie der Geschichte der Menschenheit* would have been a corrective, assigning as it did a special purpose to each secular age and each individual. But though Manzoni had

---

[35] In Bernard Weinberg, *A History of Literary Criticism in the Italian Renaissance* (Chicago: University of Chicago Press, 1961), 1:510. Weinberg cites Castelvetro's *Poetica d'Aristotle* (1576 ed.), 5, l. 21.

[36] In Weinberg, *Literary Criticism*, 1:629–30. See Tasso's *Risposta al discorso del Sig. Oratio Lombardelli* (1586).

[37] See Galletti, *Alessandro Manzoni*, 299–353.

some familiarity with the German Romantics and though Herder's ideas certainly influenced both Hegel and Manzoni's Parisian friend, Victor Cousin, Manzoni appears to bypass Herder's contribution, and perhaps because he found his views no less problematic than those of Bossuet; the problem only ran in the opposite direction. To impute as much authority as Herder did to man, above all to the historian, would be, to Manzoni, only to exchange Bossuet's providential excess for an even more misguided anthropocentrism.

The historiography of Vico achieved the balance that clearly appealed to Manzoni the most. Here was a belief that history realizes in the course of time an Idea already engraved in the mind of God, but it was a providentialism tempered by no less a belief in individual human responsibility. A view that history is not guided every step of the way by God, but committed as well to the psychology of human choice for its full realization, is one Manzoni clearly could share. His dramas and novels, not to mention his critical writings, show as much. Manzoni no more than Vico allowed, much less insisted, that the author play the part of God. Neither took understanding divine Providence to be critical to understanding the general principles governing human conduct.

If Manzoni departed at all from Vico's philosophy of history, it was to turn in a less rhetorical direction, away from its emphasis upon theoretical coherence and toward a closer correspondence to fact. When he undertook in his early *Discorso sopra alcuni punti della storia longobardica* to identify the outstanding historians of the Middle Ages, Manzoni would rank alongside Vico the more traditional Lodovico Muratori, a scholar known for his careful accumulation and presentation of fact:

> Looking to the works of Muratori and Vico, one seems to see, with combined admiration and displeasure, two great disunited forces and, at the same time, something like a glimmer of the great result that would be produced by their union.[38]

The *Discorso,* Manzoni's first and in the end greatest contribution to Italian historiography, attempted just such a synthesis. The ac-

---

[38] Manzoni, *Discorso sopra alcuni punti della storia longobardica,* in *Opere varie,* 504.

count of Charlemagne's eighth-century conquest of the Lombards perfectly abounds in historical detail. What saves it from being just a narrow if well-documented historical study is the breadth of its commentary on justice, political oppression, and individual free will.

Manzoni used the technique with even greater originality and success in his early tragedies. The plot of *Il conte di Carmagnola* closely parallels the life and, in Manzoni's view, unjust execution for treason of a fifteenth-century soldier of fortune. Evidently the story was carefully researched; as if to assure his readers of this, Manzoni supplied a special explanatory note containing historical information not included in the drama as such. Just as evidently, Manzoni selected a story to illustrate a general theme—innocence buckling under the weight of sheer political power—that projected easily on Italy's national political scene. The *Adelchi* shows a similar coupling, but of even more meticulous historical research (the *Discorso* would serve as the *Adelchi*'s historical supplement). And if anything, its theme is more pointed, namely, a race conquered and oppressed by vastly more powerful neighboring forces.

Manzoni's dramas illustrate well enough the importance he attached to a historical poetry. But it is only in the critical essays he was writing at the same time that he made his stand clear. The essays also show in a way that his dramas never could how distinctive was Manzoni's position among the Romantics. Although he readily accepted (at least within the limits I have described) the new philosophical stature of history, he rejected more and more vigorously in the course of his career rhetoric's more sophistic possibilities. He would not only take a stand against the by now fossilized classical unities, he would eschew any artistic procedure that promoted coherence at the expense of a correspondence to truth. This rejection spelled at once a rejection of the classical unities and the Romantic doctrine of the imagination.[39] Even though the classical rules of art and the doctrine of the imagination could hardly be more distinct in their insistence upon rules, on the one hand, and upon genial creation on the other, both valorized the merely human, not the

[39] This attitude is evident in several essays and letters throughout Manzoni's career: the *Lettre à M. Chauvet*, the *Lettre à V. Cousin*, and *On the Historical Novel*.

more apparently objective, absolute truths of history or religion. In this they were, for Manzoni, equally arbitrary, equally erroneous.

Thus, at a time when almost every other Romantic critic was building his theories around the doctrine of the artistic imagination, Manzoni built his around an adherence to history that was scrupulous in every respect. History, he thought, provided the most objective, sacred, and necessarily social basis for literary art to be found. The essays Manzoni wrote in this period sought, among other things, to argue this case.

Manzoni's Early Essays

Compared to *On the Historical Novel,* Manzoni's early essays are more particularized attempts at literary theory. They address one or more specific questions: the structure of historical tragedy, the inadequacy of the classical unities, the definition of Italian Romanticism. Even so, they are broadly suggestive in their implications. If they exude a certain overall optimism about the likely success of his literary ventures, they also betray an awareness of the challenges facing any poet who would draw themes and facts from history.

Take, for instance, the rationale Manzoni gives in the first of his critical essays, the preface to *Il conte di Carmagnola,* for attaching historical notes to the drama:

> I place before the tragedy some historical information about the character and the facts that are its subject, thinking that whoever decides to read a composition mixing invention and historical truth wants to be able, without lengthy research, to discover what real events lie behind it.[40]

The passage already contains what will become standard fare in the essays to follow: first, the unavoidable mixture of history and invention in any historical poetry, and second (and in apparent ten-

---

[40] Manzoni, preface to *Il conte di Carmagnola,* in *Opere varie,* 225.

sion, if not at cross-purposes, with the first) the poet's compelling urge to communicate with complete truthfulness with his audience. Of course, the very decision to provide a historical note on matters that would not fit in the drama suggests that there may be difficulties in producing historical art, even though Manzoni does not yet acknowledge them. It would seem from the passage that whatever difficulties there are may be overcome by the device of a well-researched historical supplement. The fact is that at this point in Manzoni's career as an Italian Romantic, providing a reasoned refutation of the classical unities was the more pressing business.

The *Lettre à M. Chauvet* was a response to a Paris review of *Il conte di Carmagnola*.[41] For the most part, it is a polemic against the classical unities. But by this time Manzoni's reliance upon history as the organizing principle of historical poetry is everywhere apparent. He as much as equates the "historical" with the "Romantic," using the first term interchangeably with the second.[42] Manzoni's radical preference for history cannot, of course, be evaluated apart from its premises; if truth, after all, is an ultimate value, and if history is the one source of truth, to the exclusion of both conventional rules and poetic imagination, then Manzoni's conclusion is more than justified. In fact, Manzoni not only believed that the unities were false rules of art, pretending to a universality they lacked; he further maintained that they did positive harm, coercing the author to allegorize where he might have presented individual characters, to propound moral codes where he might have probed individual acts of will.[43]

But, one might ask of Manzoni, what is gained by releasing the author from the grips of the classical unities, only to subjugate him to the dictates of history? The question is a good one because, for all that would appear, Manzoni would have him step out of one straitjacket into another, albeit of concrete rather than abstract design.

What Manzoni means by history at this point in his writing, however, is more or less what he produced in the *Discorso*, that is,

[41] Written in 1820, the letter was published in Paris in 1823.

[42] Specifically, Manzoni describes the historical system as the system that "rejects the two unities" and seeks its plot action in "reality."

[43] Manzoni, *Lettre à M. Chauvet*, 353.

documented facts as interpreted and shaped by more universal principles of human thought. In a passage of the *Lettre à M. Chauvet* clearly evoking Kant, he proposes that historian and poet share a single methodology that would consist of organizing facts around categories already found in the human mind, such as cause and effect, space, and time. Likewise, poet and historian both should sort through the facts "so as to present them in the order that the mind enjoys discovering and for which it carries the pattern in itself." [44] Still, given Manzoni's standards, the freedom that inheres in the act of sorting should not be exaggerated, confined as it is by the facts that history records. To invent facts would be to introduce elements no less arbitrary, no more grounded in truth, and ultimately no more poetic than the classical unities themselves.

Assuming that history so conceived does confine the writing of poetry as fully as the writing of history, what then distinguishes the two kinds of work? The difference for Manzoni, it would appear, is a subtle difference in field. If the historian's proper subject is history, the poet's is the interstices of history:

> If one takes away from the poet what distinguishes him from a historian, the right to invent facts, what is left? Poetry; yes, poetry. For what, in the end, does history give us? Events that are known only, so to speak, from the outside, what men have done. But what they have thought, the feelings that have accompanied their decisions and their plans, their successes and misfortunes, the words by which they have asserted—or tried to assert—their passions and wills on those of others, by which they have expressed their anger, poured out their sadness, by which, in a word, they have revealed their individuality: all that, more or less, is passed over in silence by history: and all that is the domain of poetry. [45]

This then is historical poetry, the synthesis of history and poetry that Manzoni envisions as the centerpiece of Romantic drama. If this synthesis is better articulated, more textured than in the brief preface to *Il conte,* it still shares completely that original optimism.

[44] Manzoni, *Lettre à M. Chauvet,* 317.
[45] Manzoni, *Lettre à M. Chauvet,* 345.

No more here than in the preface does Manzoni acknowledge the tension between producing a historical poetry and discharging a duty to communicate the truth. On the contrary, his plea for historical poetry seems to be predicated precisely upon an assumed harmony between the two.

The poet's exploitation of history (for Manzoni would not hesitate to call it such) also taps the natural interest of his audience in "discovering what there is in man's nature that is real and intimate, in seeing the effects of external phenomena."[46] His gains, though, are more than immediate, more than a present success. Reading between the lines, the poet's use of history, like any good investment, actually increases his opportunities for future returns. The more the public knows of history, Manzoni assumes, the more it will like it, at the continuing expense of fiction. Just as naturally, the author will respond with new and additional historical subjects and thus still more opportunity to appeal. What better authorial strategy than one that enlarges the author's scope for intellectual and even ethical effect? For surely that is what the poet gains above all else. He can loosen his bondage to the perennial love dilemmas that formed the staple of neoclassical literature ("the passion of love being of all the passions the most fertile in brisk, rapid incidents and always most susceptible to being enclosed in the narrow framework of a rule") and engage the far greater range of human experience and values that the infinite variety of history affords.[47]

History, for Manzoni, frees the audience no less than the poet. The dramatist who can play upon the natural interest in history among his public does not have to conscript it into service, forcing it to identify with the passionate delirium of the tragic actors on stage. He can leave the spectators in the audience where they belong, with their distance and their dignity:

> By having us participate in events that do not interest us as actors, where we are only witnesses, the poet can help us learn the habit of focusing our thoughts on the calm and grand ideas that efface themselves and disappear in the shock of life's

[46] Manzoni, *Lettre à M. Chauvet*, 346.
[47] Manzoni, *Lettre à M. Chauvet*, 355.

everyday realities, and that, if more carefully cultivated and made more present to mind, would doubtless better assure us our wisdom and our dignity.[48]

In the *Lettre à M. Chauvet* Manzoni thus defends historical poetry on social as well as intellectual grounds. He effectively makes historical poetry the key to a mutually beneficial relationship between dramatist and audience whereby each cedes greater freedom to the other while acquiring greater freedom for himself.[49] With this nineteenth-century transformation of the Aristotelian tradition, Manzoni produced a defense of historical poetry—indeed of all works mixing history and invention—that could reconcile rhetorical unity with historical truth and social responsibility. This theoretical union of history and poetry eventually proved less durable than it first appeared. But it was brilliant and bound to hearten the Italian Romantics, who were eager to claim Manzoni as their own.

What it was that caused Manzoni to reassess poetry's relationship to historical truth in the years just after the *Lettre à M. Chauvet* is unclear. It may have been his sensitivity to a remark of Goethe to the effect that Manzoni was too fastidiously attached to the historically verifiable, a remark prompted by, among other things, his having so awkwardly (if truthfully) separated the characters in *Il conte di Carmagnola* into two classes, "ideal" and "historical."[50] It may have reflected Manzoni's growing Christian idealism evident already in the *Lettre*. It may have simply been the trials of composing the first version of *I promessi sposi*, an experience that put his theory to the test. Finally (though this would be in no sense inconsistent with any of the foregoing), Manzoni may have felt an intuition that the very neatness of his history-based formula excluded other equally valid forms of poetic truth. Whatever the explanation, Manzoni probed further and published a second significant critical essay that faced the tension between history and poetry

[48] Manzoni, *Lettre à M. Chauvet*, 369.

[49] In his desire to reach, touch, and free his reader, Manzoni prefigures Sartre's notion of an engaged literature in "Why Write," in *What Is Literature*, trans. Bernard Frechtman (New York: Philosophical Library, 1949), 38–66.

[50] Mario Puppo, *Poesia e verità* (Florence: G. D'Anna, 1979), 24, 34.

more squarely and moved him to what proved to be a way station between the position he took in the *Lettre* and the more complex analysis he would eventually produce in *On the Historical Novel*.

Sul romanticismo was the published version of Manzoni's letter to another, this time totally friendly critic of his *Il conte di Carmagnola*, the Marchese Cesare D'Azeglio. Freely associating himself with the Italian Romantic movement, Manzoni advances a definition of Romanticism based on the practices it rejects and those it accepts. Among the practices it rejects, he counts (1) the unities, resting as they do on an arbitrary empiricism, (2) mythology, for its idolatry of the passions, and (3) imitation of previous authors since, as Manzoni points out, the great writers of the past distinguished themselves precisely by their originality. What Romanticism holds positively is, by Manzoni's own admission, less easy to identify; but all seems to flow from a single assumption, namely, that poetry ought to propose as its subject "the true as the unique source of a noble and lasting pleasure."[51] If history is the sole foundation of truth—a view easily imputable to Manzoni on the basis of his prior writings—there is no hint of that here; it is not even mentioned. But neither has history been supplanted, at least not in so many words. Truth is simply defined in more general terms and for that reason alone becomes, if anything, more open, more capacious. It even accommodates (implausible though this might appear in the light of Manzoni's previous writings) "invention":

> I do not mean to deceive you . . . or myself . . . as to how indeterminate, vague, and vacillating is the meaning of the word "true" in its application to works of the imagination. The obvious and generic meaning cannot be applied to these works in which everyone would agree there must be the invented, which is as much as to say, the false. The true that is to be found in all of these works, *even in fable,* is therefore something different from what one ordinarily means by this word and, I would say, something not defined; nor does defining it seem to me to be very easy, if indeed possible at all.[52]

[51] Manzoni, *Sul romanticismo*, in *Opere varie*, 617.
[52] Manzoni, *Sul romanticismo*, 618.

Of course, Manzoni did not introduce the element of uncertainty into poetic truth; it was always there, as far back as Aristotle's time. Indeed, Manzoni would argue, the Romantics have defined and advanced poetic truth more than any previous literary school, albeit largely in a negative way. And they have given it enough positive content—in their pursuit of "the true, the good, the useful, the rational"—to place it in harmony with Christianity.[53] If anything, in Manzoni's view, can stand over and above the particulars of history, it is the more universal truth of religion. By implication, it is in that direction that the Italian Romantics should continue to look.

Sul romanticismo establishes an important loosening of history's monopolistic grip on truth, by acknowledging that invention too has a certain truth based on, or at least consistent with, universal Christian ideals. But the fact remains that the essay finds Manzoni among questions about poetic truth that he has learned to ask but cannot yet answer. *Sul romanticismo* could not realistically have been his last work on the subject. Two events in the years between 1823 and 1827 brought him still further from his initial reconciliation of history and poetry. The first was his meeting with the Catholic philosopher Antonio Rosmini, the second the completion and publication of *I promessi sposi*.[54]

Rosmini was writing well within the European idealist tradition of Plato, Augustine, Aquinas, Descartes, and Kant. This was a tradition whose reference to reason, logic, and universal truth could appeal to Manzoni's rationalist tendencies and at the same time accommodate his evolving Christian idealism. In fact, Manzoni did find the philosophy of the young Rosmini both attractive and useful, and he embraced a good deal of it almost at once.[55]

---

[53] Manzoni, *Sul romanticismo*, 619.

[54] Manzoni first met Antonio Rosmini in 1826. The first edition of *I promessi sposi* appeared in 1827, although Manzoni had begun work on the novel (critics titled the early version first *Fermo e Lucia* and, later, *Gli sposi promessi*) as early as 1821.

[55] For Manzoni's appropriation of Rosmini's ideas, see Aurelia Accame Bobbio, *Il cristianesimo manzoniano tra storia e poesia* (Rome: Edizioni di storia e letteratura, 1954), and Galletti, *Alessandro Manzoni*, 229–30. The latter points out too Manzoni's hesitation about certain aspects of Rosminianism.

As circumstances would have it, Manzoni's gravitation to Rosmini did not require him to abandon his concern with historical poetry, for just at this time he was in the midst of rewriting *I promessi sposi*. The timing was fortunate in that it had the effect of keeping poetry's relation to truth concretely before him, as he turned a page, rewrote a paragraph, even dotted an *i*. Manzoni's artistic task in *I promessi sposi* was this: to tell an invented story of two young peasants while at the same time evoking seventeenth-century Lombardy, in which the story was set, with all the historical accuracy he could muster. His determination to achieve an aesthetically perfect synthesis of historical and poetic truth was one among several motivations that led him to put the novel through a series of revisions between its initial draft in 1823 and its first publication in 1827.[56] These early revisions entailed major changes in plot, the elimination of long digressions on language and morality, and fine adjustments in the balance and nexus between history and invention. This was a labor of adding and deleting, pruning and shaping, softening and smoothing. He would have the novel meet all the demands of art and truth as he conceived them.

By the standards of most, Manzoni succeeded eminently. The novel's keen historical sense, its form growing organically from its chosen subject, its portrait of Christian morality, and its revolutionary choice of two peasants as protagonists made it the finest expression of Italian Romanticism and a great national work. Manzoni, however, was not satisfied. The year *I promessi sposi* was published, it began to undergo linguistic revisions. On one level, these were only an extension of his constant drive to perfect the novel. But they also became part of a much vaster political project, conceived as early as 1806, to produce a single national Italian language.[57]

Even as Manzoni was leaving Milan in 1827 for Florence, where he would stay long enough to begin recasting the novel in the

[56] Manzoni rewrote the original manuscript *Fermo e Lucia* in part according to the suggestions of Visconti, Grossi, and Fauriel.

[57] On the question of Manzoni's linguistic writings see Accame Bobbio, *Cristianesimo*, and Barbara Reynolds, *The Linguistic Writings of Alessandro Manzoni* (Cambridge: W. Heffer and Sons, Ltd., 1950). Reynolds cites Manzoni's letter of 1806 to Claude Fauriel as the earliest indication of Manzoni's interest in linguistic questions (p. 12).

favored Florentine usage, *I promessi sposi* was being read and reviewed abroad. Lamartine wrote to Manzoni at once, complimenting him upon his use of history and urging him to continue writing, especially in the direction sketched in the most historical portion, book 3. The same year, a warmly favorable review appeared in Goethe's journal, *Über Kunst und Altertum*. Although it was written by one of his disciples, Goethe was clearly its author.[58] But Manzoni seized upon the single criticism to be found in the overwhelming praise, which was that he had shown perhaps an exaggerated solicitude for history. The timing and authorship of the remark gave it an enormous resonance for Manzoni, enough to set him to work almost at once drafting a response to Goethe that would become *On the Historical Novel*.

The Final Phase: *On the Historical Novel*

The years Manzoni gave to writing *On the Historical Novel*, roughly between 1828 and 1850, were those in which the historical novel as a genre was reaching the peak of its popularity in Europe. Its growth, begun in England, accompanied the nationalism, industrialization, and revolutionary spirit then on the rise throughout the continent.[59] Through its focused attention on a national past, its new interest in the material conditions of life, and its frequent choice of protagonists from the middle and even the lower classes, the historical novel easily became a vehicle for strong political and social statements. At the same time, the picturesque detail that characterized works of this kind helped ensure their appeal to a broad reading public.

The historical novel was a vogue; as such it would pass, but not without leaving behind an established genre and, more important, a sense of the novel's enormous potential to bear new form and sub-

[58] Renzo Negri, "'Del romanzo storico' nel trittico manzoniano," *Forum italicum* 11 (1977); 310; Puppo, *Poesia e veritá*, 26.

[59] Lukács, *The Historical Novel*, 19–30. See also Avrom Fleishman, *The English Historical Novel: Walter Scott to Virginia Woolf* (Baltimore, Md.: Johns Hopkins University Press, 1971).

ject matter. In form, it replaced the long episodic narrative of the eighteenth-century novel with a more concise, more closely woven plot. It also introduced a concrete narrative technique, with an emphasis upon precise dates, places, and events, as well as an unprecedented volume of dialogue, all of which served to heighten the novel's dramatic effect.[60] In subject matter, the historical novel was at least as original, transforming the diffuse social character of the eighteenth-century novel into a focused historical context rich in the specifics of art, customs, and class distinctions. The historical novels of authors such as Scott and, later, Dumas, Hugo, Vigny, and their Italian imitators combined form and subject matter with grand enough effect for Manzoni, well before Lukács, to call the genre the modern equivalent of the classical epic.[61]

The proliferation of historical novels in the years between 1820 and 1850 brought in its wake the inevitable critical writings. Vigny's famous preface to *Cinq-Mars,* taking a subjectivist stance, asserted the author's right "to subordinate factual reality at times to the idea that a historical character was meant to represent," in short, to change the facts of history. The prerogative was not so readily admitted in Italy as elsewhere, and the issue was disputed well into the 1830s. Niccolò Tommaseo, for instance, urged the would-be historical novelist to choose unknown moments in history, for they would give the imagination a freer reign. P. Zajotti, writing at the same time, denounced the genre categorically as an "immoral, irrational, hybrid form, combining novel and history, false and true." [62]

But if the question of the legitimacy of the historical novel had already been posed and preliminarily answered by the time Manzoni addressed himself to it, it was far from exhausted. Looking backward from the scope and depth of *On the Historical Novel,* the

---

[60] Lukács, *The Historical Novel,* 31.

[61] Manzoni, *On the Historical Novel,* Part I. Taking up the theme from his German predecessors, Lukács also refers to the epic nature of the historical novel. See, for example, *The Historical Novel,* 35.

[62] Alfred de Vigny, preface to *Cinq-Mars* (Paris: Michel Lévy Frères, 1863), 3; Niccolò Tommaseo, "Del romanzo storico," *Antologia* 117 (1830): 40–62, cited in Fiorenza Vittori, "Stuttura e problematica del discorso manzoniano 'Del romanzo storico,'" *Italianistica* 6 (1977): 19–42; P. Zajotti, "Idee generali sul romanzo storico," *Biblioteca italiana* 173 (1820): 161–69.

views of Vigny, Tommaseo, and Zajotti, and even Manzoni's own earlier ones, seem limited by comparison. The fact that Manzoni's final essay evolved so slowly allowed it not only to accommodate the author's maturing and expanding views of art but also to benefit from certain pertinent observations that he could draw from his own era.

A "Classical" Romantic

Though Manzoni never tied his changing ideas with a tight and single string, and though changes in emphasis are at best difficult to gauge in a writer of his thorough eclecticism, these years seem to have strongly affirmed what one might term, for the sake of analysis, the more classical elements of his thinking. In method, Manzoni came to depend more than ever on logic and reason. His overall purpose, to borrow Meyer Abrams's terms in *The Mirror and the Lamp*, became if anything more pragmatic, committed to teach as well as to please his audience.[63] But more important than the subtle reinforcement of such tendencies in method or purpose are the pivotal changes that took place in Manzoni's ideas on the subjects of language and poetic invention. In both cases, these changes likewise take a direction that is classical, but classical in a very particular sense of the word. They mark a clear turn toward a more metaphysical view of art, one quite disposed to take up philosophy's age-old quarrel with rhetoric.

From the beginning of his artistic career, Manzoni had found the various dialects on the peninsula a troubling bar to effective communication with the Italian people; but he found them particularly so as he sought to work out the linguistic revisions of *I promessi sposi*. Manzoni, though artist above all, firmly believed that the "question of the Italian language," as it was then called, required both political and artistic solutions. While his revisions of *I promessi sposi* were an early contribution to the unity of the Italian

---

[63] Meyer Abrams, *The Mirror and the Lamp: Romantic Theory and the Critical Tradition* (New York: Norton, 1958), 15–16.

language, he addressed the political aspects of Italian unity more immediately and explicitly in the linguistic tracts of his later years. Manzoni's efforts on both fronts to forge a single national language produced the gradual unfolding of a linguistic theory that would bear importantly on his final views of art.

Throughout the length of his writings, Manzoni described language as a system of signs for the communication of ideas.[64] They carry intellectual, not emotive meaning; they are ordained by usage and social convention rather than individual genius; they serve as common coin. This was not to deny the possibility of achieving artistic style. That could come as well from the skillful manipulation of linguistic convention as from the genial creation of neologisms; and if it did, it would have an advantage not shared by a subjective, self-enclosed utterance, for it could readily communicate.

While Manzoni's views on language remained basically stable throughout the long course of his career, his thinking on one point changed in a way that proved absolutely crucial to his aesthetics. That point is the relationship of language to thought. In 1831, Manzoni still espoused a basically nominalist attitude toward language. He believed that words precede and generate ideas and themselves derive from either social convention or direct sensory experience. His views on language were thus bound to be strictly rhetorical, tied to "truth," as we have seen, by the slippery bonds of an author's intention and an audience's belief. But Manzoni's reading and correspondence with Rosmini exposed him to a different, more realist view, according to which thought is ceded a reality of its own and language reduced to an index of things, a secondary aid to reflection and knowledge.[65] Although Manzoni at first resisted this view, it appears that by 1836, and largely due to Rosmini's inspiration, he was prepared to abandon nominalism altogether and acknowledge the existence of two kinds of linguistic truth: one grounded in a verbal correspondence to verifiable fact or convention, the other grounded in a verbal correspondence to Platonic ideas whose essence could only be intuited. While Manzoni con-

[64] Galletti, *Alessandro Manzoni*, 513–55. Also Reynolds, *The Linguistic Writings*.
[65] Accame Bobbio, *Cristianesimo*, 82–83.

tinued to believe that the best style was one that manipulated the supply of words already in currency, he now recognized that ideas may occasionally arise that are so new that words do not yet exist to express them. This is generally the case with poetic language, since poetry so frequently reflects a new and different vision from that common to everyday discourse. But new coinage or old, language should still serve as a transparent medium, obediently communicating the essence of a thought.[66]

A similar change was to take place in Manzoni's conception of poetic invention, though he nowhere draws an explicit connection between the two developments. As recently as 1821, in the *Lettre à M. Chauvet,* he dismissed invention as wholly subjective, arbitrary, without, so to speak, any truth to tell. But by the time he wrote *On the Historical Novel,* Manzoni had evidently come to believe in an ideal plane of truth to which invention would correspond in much the same way that history corresponds to verifiable fact. As Manzoni explained in *Dell'invenzione,* a dialogue he was writing during the same years as *On the Historical Novel,* invention "finds" an innate idea whose origin is God; it never "creates."[67] Doubtless, Manzoni had been groping toward some such notion when he wrote in *Sul romanticismo* of a "literary" truth. From *On the Historical Novel* forward, Manzoni would refer to this purely ideal plane of truth as the realm of "invention" or preferably, because invention in the historical novel had to imitate and blend with the historically verifiable, "the verisimilar":

> For the verisimilar (the raw material of art), once offered and accepted as such, becomes a truth that is altogether different from the real, but one that the mind perceives forever, one whose presence is irrevocable.[68]

Manzoni may or may not have meant to give credit to Aristotle by using the term "verisimilar." But there is no question that in recognizing a duality between history and invention, Manzoni was

---

[66] Manzoni's concept of language in many ways exemplifies Michel Foucault's description of linquistic classicism in *The Order of Things,* ed. R. D. Laing (New York: Pantheon Books, 1970), 46–77.

[67] Alessandro Manzoni, "Dell'invenzione," in *Opere varie,* 699–701 especially.

[68] *On the Historical Novel,* Part I.

taking up a standard feature of Aristotelian thought. If anything, his logic was more rigid since he had, in his typically eclectic fashion, made of Aristotle's plane of probability or necessity a separate ideal truth distinctly reminiscent of Platonism.[69] Only this way could he rid the poetic of any trace of subjectivity, leaving it as objective, as external as the concrete world of history itself.

If Manzoni's acceptance of an ideal, nonhistorical truth overcame his excessively narrow view of poetry, its metaphysical aspects introduced their own problems. For one, it disturbed the well-wrought synthesis set out in the *Lettre à M. Chauvet* according to which poetry and history remain comfortably grounded in one and the same historical truth. That was no longer tenable. More serious, Manzoni's new definitions burdened historical poetry with added aesthetic and ethical complexities. How can two such distinct levels of truth be merged without compromising the integrity of each of them? But how can they be distinguished without destroying the artistic unity of the whole? The tension between historical fact and ideal invention that Manzoni had been able to accept in his preface to *Il conte di Carmagnola* now became a flaw of intolerable dimension.

Ironically, these complexities only increase when they are grafted to Manzoni's thoroughly Romantic commitment to history. Historiography, Manzoni himself observed in his *Lettre à M. Chauvet,* was about to become a science, and it was destined to affect the literary arts profoundly.[70] By the 1840s, readers were already finding a good deal of history in narrative fiction and were demanding still more. What made matters harder for the historical poet, they also wanted to know just what sort of truth—invention or history—lay before them at any given moment.[71] The ethical burdens on the author would only grow in measure with this trend.

It may have been characteristic of Manzoni, in a contest between truth, on the one hand, and mere artistic possibility, on the other, to favor the first. But it was equally characteristic of him to

[69] The Platonic element doubtless enters Manzoni's thought through his general Christian heritage and, more specifically, through his appropriation of important elements of Rosminianism.

[70] Manzoni, *Lettre à M. Chauvet,* 368.

[71] See *On the Historical Novel,* Part I, n. 4.

postpone judgment until after examining a problem from all angles. Solutions might suggest themselves. Better yet, the conflict under close enough scrutiny might prove itself false. In the course of *On the Historical Novel*, Manzoni would come upon no ready solutions, discover no false conflict. The tension between classical and Romantic would have to play itself out fully. Not only the historical novel but all historical poetry would be implicated.

The Trial of the Historical Novel

On the Historical Novel opens with an epigraph from Cicero's *De legibus*: "Intelligo te, frater, alias in historia leges observandas putare, alias in poemate" ("I see very well, my brother, that you would have certain rules observed in history, and others in poetry"). Recalling an introductory exchange between Quintus and Marcus on the problem of distinguishing historical truth from poetry, the reference is thematically apt. That its source is Cicero—statesman, ethical philosopher, rhetorician—makes it doubly so.

For Cicero, of course, the power of human discourse and therefore of the orator traversed all matters—historical, philosophical, and poetic—on which one might speak. However, at the same time that he appreciated the power of language to express various truths, to achieve different effects, Cicero appreciated the dangers of contradiction and duplicity. Manzoni, with his accumulated artistic experience and commitment to truth, felt these rhetorical problems just as deeply, but with a difference. If they proved for Cicero a challenge to linguistic power, they were for Manzoni above all a risk. He could scarcely acknowledge the power of rhetoric without feeling responsible for its use, hence the need to curb it. Truth was the logical control. In Manzoni's view, it was also the only means to teach.

On the Historical Novel is suffused with an extraordinary solicitude for the reader. As early as in the *Lettre à M. Chauvet*, Manzoni had elevated the audience from spectator, in the most passive connotation of the term, to a companion of the author, joining him as he considers events and judges them. In *On the Historical Novel*,

the reader returns ubiquitously. He begins more as a witness than
anything else. Almost without our noticing it, he becomes judge of
the legitimacy of the historical novel; in the end he also judges its
literary ancestors, each according to the standards of its time.

Part I finds the reader serving as Manzoni's narrative device
for stating the two chief, and opposite, criticisms of the historical
novel. According to some readers, the genre fails to instruct since it
leaves them wondering which of the events described are real and
which are invented. It does not communicate an accurate correspondence to the truth. In fact, it confuses and deceives. For other
readers, however, the historical novel distinguishes history and invention all too clearly, eliminating any possibility of a unified belief
in the narrative or of the aesthetic pleasure that such a belief produces. Taking the criticisms together, the condemnation is total, for
while the genre may have set out in good Horatian fashion to instruct and delight its readers, in the end it can do neither. The historical novel ultimately is "but a species of a false genre which includes all compositions that try to mix history and invention." Like
all such flawed species, it does not have long to live; the fact that it
is "the most modern . . . refined and ingenious" among them is of
no consequence.[72]

At the same time that he condemned the historical novel and
its ancestors, Manzoni reserved approval and even praise for the
writing of history proper; and he did so, even though history too is
a mixture of sorts. At bottom, it contains, on the one hand, an ex-
position of historical fact and, on the other, a merely verisimilar authorial commentary marked by speculations and even admissions
of doubt:

> It might not be out of place to mention that history sometimes
> also uses the verisimilar, and can do so harmlessly if it uses it
> properly and presents it as such, thereby distinguishing it from
> the real. It can do this without impairing the narrative unity,
> for the simple reason that the verisimilar does not really try to
> become part of the narrative. It is merely suggested, advanced,
> considered, in short, not narrated on the same level as or

[72] *On the Historical Novel,* Part I.

melded with real facts, as is the case in the historical novel. . . .
When the mind becomes aware of information that arouses its
interest but that is fragmentary or lacking crucial details, it
tends to invoke the ideal. . . . History, at such moments, I
would say, abandons narrative, but only in order to produce a
better narrative. As much when it conjectures as when it narrates, history points to the real; there lies its unity.[73]

Manzoni's acceptance of history as the one and only allowable coupling of history and invention is doubly interesting. For one, it sets
his categorical rejection of any other such combination into only
sharper relief. More important, it points clearly to the probable
basis of what might be called his rhetorical complaint against the
historical novel.

Over the course of his essay, Manzoni drew a distinction
within history proper between historical narrative, on the one
hand, and the verisimilar, on the other, that strongly evokes the
modern distinction between *histoire* and *discours;* and a consideration of these modern rhetorical terms helps to probe Manzoni's
own. As defined by Émile Benveniste, these categories are merely
formal. *Histoire* is the form proper to a third person narrative of
past events expressed in the past definite tense; by contrast, *discours* denotes a first or second person form cast into the present,
perfect, imperfect, or *passé composé* tense and thereby tied to the
time and place of the narrator's telling.[74] It would appear that Manzoni had grasped the effectiveness of the formal interplay within a
history of two distinct frames of reference, one set in the narrator's
time and place, the other in the time and place of the narrated
events, well before that theme had entered modern critical discourse.[75] (This point is corroborated by Manzoni's description of
drama as the "pure verisimilar," since it lacks historical narrative.[76]

[73] *On the Historical Novel,* Part I.
[74] Émile Benveniste, *Problèmes de linguistique générale* (Paris: Gallimard,
1966), 225–50.
[75] For an excellent discussion of these modes of discourse in eighteenth- and
nineteenth-century historiography and literature, see Lionel Gossman, "History and
Literature," in *The Writing of History: Literary Form and Historical Understanding,*
ed. Robert H. Canary and Henry Kozicki (Madison: University of Wisconsin Press,
1978), 3–40.
[76] *On the Historical Novel,* Part II.

Here, each character speaks his own *discours*.) But Manzoni differs from Benveniste in one important respect, holding such interplay to be less a question of objective, linguistic analysis than of philosophical integrity. In his view, rhetorical forms are only legitimate when they correspond precisely to their respective planes of truth—either verifiable fact or ideal essence.

The writings of those historians Manzoni most admired—Vico, Voltaire, Muratori, as well as Thierry and Fauriel—confirmed, if they did not altogether generate, his belief in the validity of incorporating in works of history both the historically true and the so-called verisimilar. The key to their success was their simultaneous pursuit, through a careful use of language, of both honesty and unity. It is in one voice and tense (*histoire*) that they relate historical fact; it is in another (*discours*) that they judge events, evaluate sources, and consider the limits of knowledge. It is precisely the same careful use of *histoire* and *discours* to distinguish what is known from what is simply believed that allows Manzoni to find in works of history what he would call a rational means of maintaining authorial integrity without sacrificing the reader's unity of belief or undermining the author's persuasive power.

But the historical novel is altogether different from a history proper, and its aesthetic and ethical problems are far more complex. *Histoire* and *discours* scarcely can cooperate to "point to the real." What Manzoni so rightly perceives is that the new vogue of the historical novel rests upon a very different and quite problematic rhetorical strategy. Its unprecedented interest in the spatial and temporal context of the plot naturally gives historical events in all their descriptive detail a greater role than in any previous form of the novel. But for all its apparent historicity, the historical novel rests at bottom on invention. And it too, in order to acquire the reader's belief, must be produced in the form of *histoire* and woven with history proper into an integral and lifelike narrative. As Manzoni looked about him at the numerous translations and imitations of Walter Scott, he could see that for long stretches, history and invention were operating together under the cloak of *histoire*, in a way that, from a twentieth-century perspective, seemed nicely to prefigure the objectivity of the great realistic novel to follow. In the historical novel, that is, the balance between *histoire* and *discours* weighs more heavily than before in the direction of *histoire*. There is somewhat less opportunity for authorial commentary; and when the narrator does speak up, he cannot under any circumstances tell the truth about the events and characters upon which the novel is based. In this situation, the two rhetorical forms, *histoire* and *discours,* can no longer be made to correspond to Manzoni's dual dimensions of truth. History and invention become instead willfully opaque, *histoire* lending to invention the mask of history and to the narrator the guise of an honest historian.

The aesthetic and ethical difficulties facing the historical novel did not, as Manzoni himself would document, begin with that genre. Later in the essay, he would trace them as far back as the classical epic. Then too, novelists ever since Cervantes had played *histor* and bard, producing all sorts of combinations of history and invention; and the fashion had grown only stronger with the eighteenth-century novel, in which the novelist, like an actual historian, would deal personally with his reader in language that, in modern rhetorical terms, would be called *discours*.[77]

But if the historical novel did not exactly usher in the aesthetic and ethical difficulties Manzoni noted, it heightened them dramatically. When the early novelist played *discours* off against *histoire,* he did so only to accentuate the artistic character of his work. He was indeed playing, and everyone knew that. The situation of the historical novelist is quite different, for he very nearly pretends to be the *histor,* to give the reader a faithful representation of the past.[78] Worse yet, he does so through a form chosen precisely for its strong outward resemblance to history, that is, for its capacity to deceive. In distorting the truth-telling collaboration of *histoire* and *discours* that works so impeccably in well-done histories, the historical novelist does nothing less than counterfeit history itself. By these standards, the ethical burden he shoulders is enormous.

If Part I of *On the Historical Novel* deals synchronically with the genre as such, Part II sets it in diachronic perspective. Here Manzoni traces the origins of the novel to the epic and the historical tragedy. The evolution of these two literary forms into the his-

[77] Gossman, "History," 22–23.
[78] See *On the Historical Novel,* Part I.

torical novel evokes cultural transformations strongly reminiscent of Vico's *Scienza nuova*. Besides supplying Manzoni with the outlines of a providential history that pursues human rationality and perfection, Vico also supplied him with a peculiarly cyclic sense of time and the succession of ages: a poetic "age of gods," a fabulous "age of heroes," and a historical "age of man."[79] Lastly, the *Scienza nuova* gave Manzoni an optimal model for tracing the interplay of the social, political, and poetic elements that he wanted to build into his literary history. That would allow criticism to put text and author into concrete historical contexts and fully admit reader assessment. Manzoni makes the essay a literary history that is no less sociopolitical in its orientation than was his view of the historical novel and his overall theory of language. In short form, the history goes like this:

Both the authors and the audience of ancient Greece and Rome were quick to identify fables, or what Manzoni calls "the primitive or spontaneous epic," with history.[80] They were not apt to find fault with fables for mixing history with invention. But whether it realizes it or not, an audience that is unable to distinguish history from invention can easily become the object of political manipulation. Such, implies Manzoni, was precisely the effect of the earliest epics on the founding of Rome:

> The earliest form in which that story came down to us was strictly as history, and it appears that it was only a short time, if ever at all, in the hands of the cyclic poets. The original form was, as Vico said of ancient Roman law, a *serious poem*. This seems right, for it is unlikely that the patricians—the consummate keepers, preservers, and consecrators—would have left the story of the founding of those institutions by which they maintained their power over the plebes in the hands of entertainers and masters of the plebes.[81]

[79] Giambattista Vico, *The New Science*, trans. Thomas Bergin and Max Frisch (Ithaca, N. Y.: Cornell University Press, 1970), bk. 4, 281–347. Manzoni refers to Vico directly in the course of his essay.

[80] *On the Historical Novel*, Part II.

[81] *On the Historical Novel*, Part II.

At a certain point in history—Manzoni does not locate it precisely—the reader ceases to expect historical truth from poetry, but this would hardly bring the writing of epics to an end. In the absence of a modern science of history, capable of refuting poetic renditions of a given historical event, epics could still be written and enjoyed for their beauty and interest alone. This was perhaps one of historical poetry's most propitious moments, and it produced Manzoni's poetic ideal, Vergil's *Aeneid*.

The founding of Rome was the perfect subject. Being mythological, it did not invoke history proper; but having in its background a major event in secular history, it had genuine sociopolitical appeal. Not that subject matter alone made the *Aeneid* great. In the final analysis, it was Vergil's use of language. Manzoni devotes some of the most moving lines of his work to explaining how Vergil's powerful style made the tale unforgettable:

> It makes little difference whether inventions are old or new, as long as they have passed through the hands of Vergil.
>
> The reason is that Vergil's poetic style is simply unsurpassed in power. By poetic style, I mean the style that distinguishes itself from common usage by its advantage—and a very important one for anyone who exploits it—in expressing ideas that common language is not called upon to express, but that still deserve to be expressed once they have been conceived. . . . *He speaks almost another language,* because he has such different things to say. . . .
>
> Rarely does he do this, and even more rarely with much success, by inventing new words as scientists do. Almost invariably, it is by combining usual words in unusual ways.[82]

It was not out of simple economy that Vergil built his poetic idiom with everyday words. He knew that expressing new intuitions through syntactic play on the familiar—"making strange" in the Shklovskian sense—achieves a stylistic *écart* of which new coinage is utterly incapable.[83] It "effectively increases our knowledge,"

[82] *On the Historical Novel,* Part II.
[83] See Negri, "'Del romanzo storico' nel trittico," 322, for a discussion of Manzoni's literary debt to Vergil's method.

Manzoni would say, counting the *Aeneid* proof perfect of what had come to be his own linguistic ideal.

The advent of the historical sciences still had to be reckoned with. Although Manzoni could only welcome the knowledge of history that came with what Vico called "historical" times, the demands of a knowledgeable readership were, as we have seen, difficult to satisfy, even for an author willing and able to supply historical detail in quantity. The epic form could not expand to take in so much history gracefully. Forcing historical matter into an older, canonized form was awkward in the extreme, as Silius Italicus's attempts amply show. But to avoid historical themes in historical times as Valerius and Statius did was to render the epic empty and lackluster.[84]

Epics continued to be written well into the eighteenth century, but after Torquato Tasso, Manzoni believes, the public no less than the authors lost interest in them. "The public wanted to call the writing of such poems to a halt."[85] Those that did follow, such as Voltaire's *La Henriade,* show history's toll on their face; they are reduced to carrying a preamble before them as testimony to a historical truth that their fossilized forms could not comfortably contain.

Manzoni also traces the impact of history on tragedy, although in much less detail. Perhaps he thought the epic had already made his case; more likely, he felt he had dealt adequately with the drama in his earlier essays. Apart from its brevity, this section is most striking for Manzoni's account of why tragedy can shield itself so much more effectively than the epic from the encroachments of history. The primary reason is formal, even rhetorical. Since tragedy, by definition, does not rely upon historical narrative, since history proper is not so fully woven into its linguistic fabric as in the case of the epic, tragedy is less easily undone. History would not exert its full effect until Manzoni's own day, when it finally displaced the classical unities as the organizing principle of drama. By way of the historical tragedy, Manzoni quickly returns to the historical novel,

[84] *On the Historical Novel,* Part II.
[85] *On the Historical Novel,* Part II.

only the most recent literary device for joining history and invention, and one with some real advantages over the epic and the historical tragedy.

To be sure, "The historical novel does not suffer, as do the epic and the tragedy . . . from that coarse fiction that consists of packing a true, celebrated, and therefore necessarily important event with fables."[86] Its principal subject, after all, "is completely the author's, completely poetic, because merely verisimilar." But it labors, in a way, under worse handicaps. By now, both author and reader are in possession of truths they did not have before:

> What differentiates us from people of those times [the poetic pagan ages] is the possession of a historical criticism that seeks the real truth in past facts and, what is so much more important, the possession of a religion which, being the truth, cannot conveniently be adapted to arbitrary changes and fanciful elaboration. Is this something to complain about?[87]

In the end, the historical novel is surely in no better situation than epic and tragedy, and probably in worse. Its demise is inevitable. Manzoni contents himself, by way of epitaph, with affirming the verdict reached in Part I:

> In fact, the two opposite criticisms that furnished the lines of argument for the trial of the historical novel had already showed up in the first moments of the genre and at the height of its popularity, like germs of an eventually mortal illness in a healthy-looking baby.[88]

I promessi sposi: A Memorial to a Genre

Manzoni's entirely pessimistic predictions for the historical novel were surprisingly accurate. By 1850, the year that *On the*

---

[86] *On the Historical Novel,* Part II.
[87] *On the Historical Novel,* Part II.
[88] *On the Historical Novel,* Part II.

Historical Novel first appeared, the genre was already in decline. As literary history unfolded, the historical novel turned out to have been but a signpost, albeit a major one, on the way toward the great realistic novel that dominated the literary scene more or less until the turn of the century. Its particular legacy to the realistic novel was a narrative rhetoric steeped in *histoire* and grounded in causal-chronological patterns evocative of what we take to be history.

However short-lived the genre, *I promessi sposi* as a work plainly has survived. Although it has been for a long time critical cant that *On the Historical Novel* was a condemnation of *I promessi sposi,* the essay makes no critical reference to Manzoni's own novel.[89] In fact, there is positive ground to believe that Manzoni felt optimistic about *I promessi sposi,* if not the genre to which it belonged. In the first place, the essay itself allows that certain works may attain a poetic immortality though written in genres that do not last:

> When I said before that the chivalric epic died, did I deny that the *Furioso* has lived on? Did Tasso, when he insisted that "the subject of the heroic poem be drawn from history of not too remote an age," mean to remove the *Aeneid* from the ranks of living poems because its subject came from the age of fables, a time very remote even for Vergil? Certainly not. Tasso was not referring to what had already been done, but to what could be done again.[90]

Manzoni may well have hoped that *I promessi sposi* would be for the historical novel what the *Furioso* and the *Aeneid* were for the chivalric and the literary epic, respectively, that is, a work that would survive the genre in which it was written. The novel had the makings of such a work. Its subject matter was well chosen and sufficiently historical to match the needs of its times, and the novel

[89] Although I do not agree completely with his views, Pietro Viola, in "Il discorso manzoniano 'Del romanzo storico,'" *Convivium* 36 (1968), 665–731, does offer a modern reevaluation of Manzoni's essay and, in particular, its relationship to *I promessi sposi*. Of course, in order to gain a full understanding of the relationship between *I promessi sposi* and Manzoni's theory of the novel, one would have to consider as well his other essays, his letters to Fauriel, and the *Materiali estetici*.

[90] *On the Historical Novel*, Part II.

form was flexible enough to accommodate it. From a linguistic point of view, *I promessi sposi,* especially the final edition, put vigorously into practice all the well-considered linguistic standards Manzoni had prescribed in his writings on the Italian language. In fact, and still speaking of style, the novel bore a close affinity to the *Aeneid.* That Manzoni emulated the great master is almost obvious. It is not simply that he devoted a long section of his essay to Vergil; it is that he borrowed his techniques. Like Vergil, Manzoni would "speak almost another language" and manage to do so "by combining usual words in unusual ways."[91]

Equally important, the novel was constructed in such a way as to mitigate the aesthetic and ethical problems that Manzoni considered endemic to its genre. It is true that the novel contains vast quantities of historical fact, far more than most other novels, and this by itself might suggest that the problems would be so much the greater. But Manzoni also included long passages of *discours,* in which he addresses the reader directly and puts him at a knowing distance from the events described. If Manzoni's way of combining *histoire* and *discours* was to superimpose an expanded personal commentary upon long historical accounts, its product was a highly textured, closely woven narrative that would deceive or jar as little as possible. That such a narrative would minimize deception is clear. The unity would come from the balancing act of *histoire* and *discours.* It is in fact the clear demarcation between the two that lends *I promessi sposi* the pronounced irony for which it is known. The assertion of a strong authorial presence, with its own well-defined ideological perspective, allows the author to comment fully and with sustained detachment upon the events narrated in *histoire.*

The rigor of Manzoni's authorial commentary is strengthened by the fact that he manufactured it not out of general historical maxims inserted here and there to explain or ease the progress of an invented plot, as was the practice of many novelists who came before.[92] His *discours* invoked actual historical documentation, chal-

---

[91] See Negri, "'Del romanzo storico' nel trittico," 321–23.

[92] See Gerard Genette, "Vraisemblance et motivation," in *Figures II* (Paris: Editions du Seuil, 1969), 71–98, for the role of authorial commentary in the "motivation" of a verisimilar text.

lenging the reader to verify in its light the ideal truthfulness of the story being told. A good example comes as early as chapter 1:

> On his head each [bandit] wore a green net hanging over the left shoulder and ending in a large tassel; from this net a heavy lock of hair fell over their foreheads. They had long mustachios curled up at the ends; shining leather belts on which hung a brace of pistols; a small powder-horn dangled like a locket on their chests; the handle of a knife showed from a pocket of their loose wide breeches; they had rapiers with big, gleaming, furbished hilts of pierced brass, worked in monograms. It was obvious at first glance that they were men of the class known as bravoes.
>
> This class, now quite extinct, was then very flourishing in Lombardy, and was already of considerable antiquity. Here, for the reader who may know little about it, are a few genuine examples, which may give an idea of its chief characteristics, of the efforts made to exterminate it, and of its vigorous and obstinate vitality.[93]

And there follow two and a half pages with quotations from sixteenth- and seventeenth-century documents describing the historical class that Manzoni's characters represented. Thus authorial commentary draws openly from the records of history to make its invention believable, to make it seem an ideal example of a general factual condition. Manzoni's use of the technique peaks in the chapters on the plague.

The strategy I have described took the historical novel about as far as it could go in overcoming the difficulties Manzoni saw in what he called trying to "put the original and the portrait into a single work."[94] Still, as *On the Historical Novel* plainly shows, Manzoni's success in *I promessi sposi* did not ultimately dissuade him from believing that the genre was fatally flawed. His disenchantment was so strong that the *Storia della colonna infame*, the work he published just after *I Promessi sposi,* but which began as a

dro Manzoni, *The Betrothed*, trans. Archibald Colquhoun (New :965), 3.
Historical Novel, Part II.

long digression within it, was, not a novel at all, but a judicial-style narrative inquiry, informed by well-documented research and conducted by a dramatized narrator with a strong ideological bent. There Manzoni was the *histor,* authentically and unambiguously. With it he began another writing career, one that dropped the idea of a fictional plot. This, he felt, put him more in step with the demands of his age, or, more precisely, with truth in the way his age defined it.

Manzoni's last years were particularly difficult ones, bringing the death of his second wife as well as of five of his seven children. Nonetheless, he continued to write: essays, dialogues, two historical narratives. Though they never attained the popularity of *I promessi sposi,* they kept him at the forefront of Italian letters and, since letters were then so closely bound to the question of Italian independence, as close as ever to the Italian political scene.

As long as the Austrians dominated the peninsula, Manzoni had refused all official honors offered him. But with the unification in 1861 and the eventual establishment of the capital at Rome, he was ready to respond to the Italy he loved. He had already been named Senator of the Kingdom in 1860, and in 1868 he accepted the presidency of a commission to study the question of the Italian language. He fulfilled his task admirably, publishing his *Dell'unità della lingua e dei mezzi di diffonderla* and *Intorno al vocabulario.* In 1872, he was granted honorary Roman citizenship, and by the time he died in 1873, Manzoni had become something of a national institution. He was visited by the likes of Gladstone, Longfellow, Newman, Pedro II of Brazil, and Balzac, to name a few. He had, moreover, seen many of the dreams he had worked for come true. He had watched a united Italy come into existence. He had worked for a united Italian language, a program for which would be established in the next decade largely on the basis of his own writings. He had labored to write the truth as he saw it and as he thought befit the ages in which he lived.

On the Historical Novel Today

In the years since Manzoni's death, interest in his work has fluctuated greatly, even in Italy itself. His near contemporaries—including writers such as Tommaso Grossi, Massimo D'Azeglio, Cesare Cantù, and Giulio Carcano—considered *I promessi sposi* a model for their own endeavors.[95] But toward the turn of the century, as the literary ideals of Romanticism were becoming exhausted, the Italian avant-garde began to experiment with new and, whenever possible, unconventional language and themes. For writers of this persuasion, such as the influential "Scapigliati milanesi," Manzoni's plain-speaking prose and historical realism held little interest. It was only in the period of the two world wars, and particularly on the eve of the second, that the literary prestige of *I promessi sposi* soared once again. Doubtless this was due in part to the novel's then very timely appeal to Italian nationalism. Beyond that, the period brought a new literary appreciation of self-conscious prose writing and traditional themes, and of these Manzoni's efforts were, of course, exemplary. Writers of the time, such as Vincenzo Cardarelli, Emilio Cecchi, and Antonio Baldini, readily acknowledged Manzoni's influence on their own discursive syntax (frequently in essaylike form) and realistic narrative content.

Today, *I promessi sposi* still has its admirers. But while it may rank as a piece of historical realism with the likes of Tolstoy's *War and Peace,* it is not now for the most part an actively influential force within the European canon. *I promessi sposi* may be saying to writers of the late twentieth century precisely what Manzoni heard the great epics say to writers of his own time: "Admire me, but do otherwise."[96]

The fortune of Manzoni's experimental narrative, the *Storia della colonna infame,* is another story altogether. In Manzoni's day, the work produced an outcry born less of active dislike than disappointed expectations. Not surprisingly, it inspired little by way of imitation. But in this case, time may have played one of its frequent tricks on critical judgment, for the twentieth century has witnessed

[95] Sapegno, *Disegno,* 575–76.
[96] *On the Historical Novel,* Part II.

literary developments in precisely the direction to which the *Storia della colonna infame* pointed.[97] The vast potential of such a narrative model would be explored in the long years since Manzoni's death, and with great popularity, by writers as diverse as André Gide, Truman Capote, Leonardo Sciascia, and Aleksandr Solzhenitsyn, the latter calling his *Gulag Archipelago* precisely "an essay of narrative inquiry."[98] There is insufficient evidence to call the *Storia* a source of these later efforts, but it does strikingly prefigure them.

Like the *Storia della colonna infame, On the Historical Novel* suffered for years from misapprehension, and it probably remains Manzoni's most neglected work. For this, Francesco De Sanctis can take large responsibility, for it was he, writing at the height of popularity of *I promessi sposi*, who proclaimed the essay to be nothing more or less than Manzoni's repudiation of his own greatest work and the death knell of his literary creativity:

> This new Tasso, in thinking over his idea, his purpose, his manner, and his result, at a time when his poetic power weakened, when the critic conquered the artist, called the whole thing into question and published his essay *On the Historical Novel;* there he tried to demonstrate that the approval it had received was the product of a vogue, that *I promessi sposi* was destined to disappear like the novels of Scudéry and, so he said, of Walter Scott. As critic, he said, "I disapprove of my novel."[99]

In recent years, several Italian critics—particularly Fiorenza Vittori, Renzo Negri, Mario Puppo, and Pietro Viola—have brought about a rediscovery of the essay. To date, however, the relationship between the ideas Manzoni developed and more current critical thought has gone unexplored. The fact is that, like the more historical *Storia della colonna infame*, whose genre it justified by implication, *On the Historical Novel* strikes some important twentieth-century chords. While the legitimacy of the historical novel as such no longer lays claim to sustained critical debate, the general questions that it raises are of continuing pertinence: the perennial rhe-

[97] See Renzo Negri, *Manzoni diverso* (Milan: Marzorati, 1976), 47–78.
[98] Negri, *Manzoni,* 72.
[99] Francesco De Sanctis, *Manzoni* (Turin: Einaudi, 1955), 257.

torical problem of history and poetry, as well as the place of the novel in literary history.

More than the nineteenth century, ours is evidently a rhetorical age, impelled by problems of language and literary strategy. Does language make its own truth—and ours? Or does it correspond strictly to something defined and absolute? Manzoni's rhetorical complaint against the historical novel, his desire to lay bare historical truth for sociopolitical ends, situates his essay at the heart of a wide-ranging twentieth-century debate.[100]

Viewing the literary text as a rhetorical phenomenon rich in sophistic potential, writers of a structuralist and poststructuralist bent over the last twenty years have formulated a nominalist view of language according to which truth lies neither in some objective reality nor in the authorial imagination, but emerges out of the process of signification. Since meaning stems from relationships within an autonomous sign system, history—in Manzoni's sense of referring to an outside reality—is, for this group of literary theorists, by definition impossible. The burden of Roland Barthes's "Le discours de l'histoire," for example, is to recast historical writing as an internal, systematic linguistic event rather than an external, referential one. According to a passage reminiscent of the classical rhetorician Gorgias (to whom Barthes, in fact, earlier refers):

> The narration of past events, commonly subjected in our culture to the sanctions of historical "science," placed under the imperious guarantee of the "real," justified by "rational" principles of exposition—does this narrative really differ, by any specific traits, from imaginary narrative such as one finds in the epic, the novel, the drama?[101]

If historical narrative is no more than a variant on the imaginary, then reality is not re-presented. "Effects of the real" are but linguistic by-products. What is then the distinctive feature of historical narrative? Nothing more than the particular sleight of hand by

---

[100] For a succinct discussion of the problem, at least as it stood in 1977, see the exchange of views between Wayne C. Booth, M. H. Abrams, and J. Hillis Miller, "The Limits of Pluralism," *Critical Inquiry,* 3 (Spring 1977): 407–47.

[101] Roland Barthes, "Le discours de l'histoire," *Information sur les sciences sociales,* 6, no. 4 (1967): 65.

which language creates the *illusion* that an external reality is being re-presented:

> "That fact" never has anything but a linguistic existence (as a term of discourse), and nevertheless all happens as if this existence were only the pure and simple "copy" of another existence, situated in an extrastructural field, the "real." The historical discourse is without doubt the only one where the referent is viewed as exterior to discourse, without it ever being possible to reach it outside of discourse.[102]

Instead of *reflecting* facts as Manzoni believed, historical narrative *creates* them. The rhetorical tables are completely turned.

Nothing better underscores the opposition between a structuralist view of historical rhetoric and Manzoni's own than Barthes's closing reference to Augustin Thierry. Thierry was to Manzoni one of the great scientific historians, and at least in part because of his narrative technique. Barthes calls him instead "chief theoretician" of the nineteenth-century illusion of history.[103]

A structuralist view of history, it must be admitted, does provide an exit from Manzoni's impasse, the later deconstructionist elaboration of the question even more so.[104] To align history and invention on a single rhetorical plane is to remove the very heterogeneity within the historical novel that started Manzoni off on his inquiry in the first place. Doing so, in turn, makes moot all problems particular to the genre, ethical no less than aesthetic.

If this view, in a sense, solves Manzoni's dilemma over the historical novel, it clearly does not do so in a way Manzoni would have approved. The solution rests upon just the sort of linguistic nominalism that he rejected and, one might say, feared religiously for much of his life. It reduces to man-made linguistic constructs, and therefore to the arbitrary, anything that might otherwise pass for truth, including those things Manzoni held to be inviolable. If structuralist and deconstructionist reasoning thus manages to make

---

[102] Barthes, "Le discours," 73.

[103] Barthes, "Le discours," 75.

[104] For a deconstructionist view of philosophical truth and the metaphors of fiction and poetry, see, for example, Jacques Derrida's "La mythologie blanche," in *Marges de la philosophie* (Paris: Editions de Minuit, 1972), 247–324.

moot one narrow ethical question, Manzoni would doubtless find that it opens an entire ethical as well as epistemological abyss. He would surely have turned his back upon such relativistic solutions, although not without arguing back. And in this attitude he would find some ready allies today. To conjecture, however briefly, about how Manzoni would position himself in contemporary literary thought, one would have to consider Meyer Abrams, Wayne Booth, and, above all, the French philosopher Paul Ricoeur.

Common to Manzoni and Ricoeur is a strong belief that the systematic quality of language ultimately depends upon an a priori referential function. No less than Manzoni, Ricoeur thus argues for distinguishing both between types of literary discourse and between types of referential truth. In fact, Ricoeur's precise concern with language as a human act deploying various levels of discourse and holding them in fruitful tension expands, albeit unintentionally, Manzoni's fundamental concern with a discourse appropriate to the historically true and the mere verisimilar into a rich philosophical frame of reference. Taking up the argument between philosophy and rhetoric directly and drawing upon Benveniste as well as upon a wide range of Anglo-American, French, and German critics, Ricoeur concludes in *La métaphore vive* that philosophical thought and poetry, not unlike Manzoni's history and poetry, operate upon two separate planes, or, as he puts it in a Hölderlin quote taken from Heidegger, "dwell upon two separate mountains."[105]

But as Manzoni makes clear in a variety of essays and particularly in *On the Historical Novel*, his concern with history has strong ethical as well as philosophical dimensions. He would, as we recall, strive to communicate fully and truthfully in order to effect social, perhaps even political, change. It is through this ethical dimension that Manzoni ultimately transcends any current rhetorical faction or school to join those writers on either side of the rhetorical fence who might today be called engaged. These authors—and I am thinking not only of Sartre, but of Foucault, Barthes in some of his early work, and Edward Said as well, to name a few—choose not to emphasize the undecidable, the unknowable in literature, but

---

[105] Martin Heidegger, *Was ist das—die Philosophie?* (Pfullingen, Neske, 1956), 45, cited by Paul Ricoeur, *La Métaphore vive* (Paris: Editions du Seuil, 1975), 398.

rather the way language exerts a power upon and within society as a whole.

More modern in content than in style, Manzoni's essay might thus be said to take a place among voices calling now for a historical and, at the same time, ethical evaluation of literature. If there is a certain universality to this long-neglected piece, it is not because it is uncompromisingly Christian or, in general, essentialist (though it is both of these), but at least in part because it calls upon the writer to be engaged to the ethics as well as the historically grounded art of communication.

But there is a surer way in which Manzoni's essay speaks to twentieth-century critical concerns. In identifying the novel's place in literary history and particularly its continuity with the epic, Manzoni presented—very early and in a remarkably systematic fashion—a frame of reference for the novel that has since become practically standard. We might single out, by way of example, the work of Georg Lukács in *The Historical Novel* and *The Theory of the Novel* and of Robert Scholes and Robert Kellogg in *The Nature of Narrative*.

It is true that Manzoni and Lukács work from premises that are in many ways philosophically diverse. While Manzoni takes the low road of what I have called a classical Romanticism, Lukács's is the high road of Hegelian idealism and, in a later phase of his career, its Marxist revision. It is also true that the question of history's relationship to poetic invention never in itself becomes a compelling issue for Lukács. But they share some philosophical sources, and many of their basic assumptions as well as specific insights are remarkably alike.

Though Lukács's place in history lends his work theoretical dimensions that Manzoni's lacks (and I think particularly of the influence on Lukács of Hegel and the neo-Kantian school), both critics reflect the dualities of thought so typical of Kant and the more important early German Romantic philosophers such as Schiller and Schlegel. Manzoni's troublesome dyad of history and invention corresponds, that is, at least on some level, to the prevalent Romantic distinction between objective fact and subjective intention. Lukács's work, with its greater reliance upon German philosophy, focuses yet more fully on the central Romantic question of subject and object—but opts in the end for the same objective qualities in art that Manzoni prefers.

Lukács never denies the subject and the subject's role in historical change and in literary works. But he does reject any radical separation of subject from the objective world, believing it is precisely their interrelationship that defines what we know as history. And history serves, for Lukács as for Manzoni, as the primary index of the reality that literature should strive to represent. In the light of this belief, Lukács, like Manzoni, tends to discount more purely subjectivist literature in favor of a more historical approach.

But what characterizes history, after all? It is, in the eyes of Lukács as of Manzoni before him, not so much a static given as a changing, moving force. Lukács's important early work, *The Theory of the Novel*, features a historicizing of aesthetic categories not very different in its general effects and even its specific insights from Manzoni's own Viconian account of narrative's changing shape and place in the course of Western history. Taking up the German Romantic notion of the novel's evolution from the epic, Lukács attempts to situate this evolution within specific historical conditions. Basing his views on the Hegelian dialectic between the subjective world of spirit and the objective world of nature, Lukács describes an evolution from a primary moment of integration, when the human being and nature are at one (the period of the epic), to a modern, more rational and philosophical moment of separation from nature (the period of the novel).

Though it would be difficult to gauge just how much Manzoni's basically Aristotelian dichotomy owes to later philosophical elaborations of subject and object, and thus how close his notions come to Lukács's frame of reference in *The Theory of the Novel*, it is perfectly clear that both Lukács and Manzoni view the novel itself as a form that is peculiarly split, dichotomous, and therefore problematic. In Lukács's view, the novel as a subjective creation can never make contact with or adequately represent the objective reality that is its major point of focus. The very struggle to regain the lost unity of subject and object is both the source of the novel's characteristic irony and of its aptitude for epitomizing the modern age. Lukács and Manzoni thus arrive at a single, unusually precise conclusion: the novel evolved from the epic and, in this process, gained a greater rationality at the expense of its former unity. Lukács concludes that the novel is the epic of an age in which the extensive totality of life has ceased to be sensuously given but which continues to think "in terms of totality"[106]—conclusions that, a hundred years before, Manzoni's essay powerfully prefigures.

This is not to suggest that the two theorists simply pass a common judgment on the evolution they describe. Whereas Lukács is frankly nostalgic for an earlier age with its unproblematic unity, Manzoni is not. (We remember Manzoni's statement that only the moderns are fortunate enough to have a clear sense of both historical and Christian truth.) And, while Lukács resigns himself to the novel's split as a sign of modernity, Manzoni quietly buries the languishing genre to which he had given so many years and declares the advent of a new, even more historical literary era.

When we turn from the novel in general to the historical novel in particular, the relationship between Lukács and Manzoni only gains complexity. The very fact that Lukács thought the form important enough to theorize about already sets him apart from most theorists of the novel. That *The Historical Novel* advances a profoundly considered theory of the form rather than merely a historical or critical discussion of it suggests that Lukács offers the only major theory of the genre besides that of Manzoni himself.

By the time Lukács wrote *The Historical Novel,* his early Hegelian viewpoint had taken a fully Marxist turn. The philosophical transformation yielded much in the way of theoretical and historical insights. Yet they are insights that again correspond in no small measure to some of Manzoni's own. A sophisticated Marxist view of history, for instance, together with the advantages of hindsight, allows Lukács to demonstrate a perfect coincidence between the short career of the historical novel and the early nineteenth century, a period of alliance between the bourgeoisie and the proletariat.[107] Remarkably, while living in the very midst of the era of the historical novel, Manzoni predicted a lifetime for it that Lukács, without apparently ever having read Manzoni's essay, independently corroborates. Less by way of corroboration than elaboration, *The His-*

---

[106] Georg Lukács, *The Theory of the Novel,* trans. Anna Bostock (Cambridge: M.I.T. Press, 1971), 56.

[107] Lukács, *The Historical Novel,* 19–88.

torical Novel also affirms an interest in the sociopolitical conditions of everyday life that Manzoni had displayed so fully both as an artist and a critic. *I promessi sposi,* which Lukács did read, he found exemplary of a proper sociopolitical consciousness:

> [Manzoni's] basic theme is much less a given, concrete, historical crisis of national history as is always the case in Scott; it is rather the critical condition of the entire life of the Italian people resulting from Italy's fragmentation, from the reactionary feudal character which the fragmented parts of the country had retained owing to their ceaseless petty internecine wars and their dependence on the intervention of the great powers. . . . Without ever departing from the concrete framework of time, place and the age- and class-conditioned psychology of the characters, the story of Manzoni's lovers grows into the tragedy of the Italian people as a whole.[108]

Manzoni doubtless would not have particularly appreciated being cited as authority for a Marxist interpretation of literature. There is no evidence that he was favorably impressed by, even very much interested in, what Marx and others were writing at that time. His expression of views on the French Revolution, but more important, his profound Christian belief in individual human choice and his fervid nationalism strongly suggest otherwise. This is not to imply that Manzoni's apparent sympathy with the plight of the oppressed as revealed by his treatment of peasant life in *I promessi sposi* was at all inauthentic. His social and political beliefs were deeply felt, even though not Marxist, not even programmatic. If there is a certain populism to the critical thinking voiced in *On the Historical Novel,* it emanates from the very public orientation of Manzoni's art and, more particularly, from his impulse to communicate openly and respectfully with a large and differentiated reading public. His attitude toward his reader is, if anything, individualistic, concerned above all with the aesthetic and ethical responsibility an author owes to each one of them. In the end, Manzoni's social consciousness concretizes itself in rhetorical questions that Lukács either does not see or does not care to address.

[108] Lukács, *The Historical Novel,* 70.

In literary critical terms, it is perhaps this attention to the author's craft that most separates *On the Historical Novel* from Lukács's important twentieth-century discussion of the form. If Lukács concerns himself with more general, more theoretical questions, Manzoni stays more consistently attuned to the actual problems of the writer as he struggles with the literary genre in which he had chosen to work. And, although this different orientation may result in part from Lukács's Hegelian and, later, Marxist orientations, with their greater tendency to treat questions of content, it also stands as the honest reflection of two very different literary personalities—one the creative writer concerned with the form that dominated his career, the other a professional philosopher and theorist.

It is not altogether surprising, perhaps, that a traditional branch of American criticism should also produce a work near in spirit to *On the Historical Novel*. For instance, although Scholes and Kellogg, in *The Nature of Narrative*, barely treat the historical novel as a separate genre, preferring to situate it as an episode in the story of the realistic novel, what they say about the development of the novel shares the tenor of Manzoni's piece.[109] They depart from the familiar Aristolelian dichotomy between the historical (or, as Scholes and Kellogg put it, empirical) dimension and the poetic (or fictional) dimension of literature, and a sense of the tension between the two.[110] What is more striking, they end up supporting Manzoni's most particular assertions. Their account follows these lines: Oral literature, almost certainly corresponding to what Manzoni meant by the literature of the "spontaneous epic," is an expression of an original, unproblematic fusion between history and poetry. It gradually degenerates, though, in postclassical times into historical studies of an empirical nature, on the one hand, and fictional or poetic creation, on the other. The novel eventually becomes the form through which artists try "to have their empirical bread and eat their fictional cake too."[111]

As their aphorism suggests, Scholes and Kellogg—like Man-

---

[109] Robert Scholes and Robert Kellogg, *The Nature of Narrative* (London: Oxford University Press, 1966).

[110] Scholes and Kellogg, *The Nature*, 12–15.

[111] Scholes and Kellogg, *The Nature*, 246.

zoni—think the effort to fuse history (or any empirical dimension of thought) and poetry inevitably problematic, documenting at a distance of one hundred years what Manzoni seems largely to have foreseen. An author must either produce a narrative that makes continual concessions to the demands of the empirical or abandon realism altogether and find a new dispensation. In words that practically restate Manzoni's own, Scholes and Kellogg write:

> The monuments of the past will remain, as Homeric epic remains, to remind us of a vanished literary medium. But the older forms of story-telling, including the great achievements of the novel's golden age—the nineteenth century—may cease to be viable for the practitioners of the narrative.[112]

The gulf that nonetheless distances the thinking of Scholes and Kellogg from Manzoni's is in great part a function of history itself. No one writing well past the mid-twentieth century is likely to see truth, beauty, and goodness the way Manzoni did. Manzoni appears to be more optimistic than both Lukács, so far as the immediacy of real sociopolitical reform is concerned, and Scholes and Kellogg, in terms of achieving empirical and poetic truth. It is curious that, while Manzoni wrote his essay *On the Historical Novel* in a period of belief in the historical methodology of Thierry and Fauriel and in the midst of a great Romantic religious revival, within a matter of years the writings of Nietzsche and Freud, among others, would begin to cast his underlying assumptions into doubt. If Scholes and Kellogg can accept with greater detachment than Manzoni the inability of the novel to reconcile its empirical and fictional tendencies, this is in part because they, like most modern critics, have come to terms with relativism, "a movement away from dogma, certainty, fixity, and all absolutes in metaphysics, in ethics and in epistemology."[113]

Being in no position to anticipate the challenge of twentieth-century thought, Manzoni could predict the breakdown of the historical novel, but not the literary forms that would take its place. Nor would he be able to predict the numerous variations of the

---

[112] Scholes and Kellogg, *The Nature*, 281.
[113] Scholes and Kellogg, *The Nature*, 276.

modern narrative as it transformed over the years, passing from the historical novel into the several forms of the realistic novel and finally splitting apart into the two separate tendencies it had tried to reconcile: the purely empirical and the purely fictional. How could Manzoni know that a reader might eventually become less interested in the reaffirmation of positive facts than in a demonstration of man's conscious—or even unconscious—fictional transformation of them? That there would be a place in literary history—and an important one—for the works of a Joyce or a Kafka?

Differences like these may be inevitable in critics separated by over one hundred years. But that Manzoni had as early as the mid-nineteenth century described the tension implicit in the novel and had related it to earlier narrative genres makes his essay a particularly apt and important entry into the open dossiers of critical thought on the nature and validity of the novel form. Compared to the range of a work such as *The Theory of the Novel, The Historical Novel,* or *The Nature of Narrative, On the Historical Novel* might be described variously as narrow and tight, dense and convoluted, or simply overly logical. Of course, Manzoni's aim was not to encompass all, or even to be broadly suggestive. And so his work glances by a variety of important issues that it itself raises, shunting them aside out of concentration on the particular genre that is the historical novel and, even more narrowly, on the dilemma facing the scrupulous writer of one. But the elements of a very modern theory seemingly are all in place. They need only to be drawn out, debated, and discussed with the energy of today's criticism.

ON THE HISTORICAL NOVEL

and, in General, on Works

Mixing History and Invention

Intelligo te, frater, alias
in historia leges observandas
putare, alias in poemate.

[I see very well, my brother,
that you would have certain
rules observed in history, and
others in poetry.]

Cicero, *De legibus*

WARNING

The author would be in a fine
predicament if he had to
establish that the ideas set
forth in the following essay
are consistent with the letter
[the *Lettre à M. Chauvet*]
that precedes. He can only say
that, if he has changed his
opinion, it was not in order
to turn backward. But whether
his move forward has been a step
toward truth or a fall into
error, the reasonable reader
can judge for himself, if he
thinks that the subject and
work warrant judging at all.

PART I

The historical novel is subject to two different, in fact, two diametrically opposite criticisms; and since these go to the very essence of the genre rather than mere secondary qualities, it seems that to identify and examine them is a good way, perhaps the best way to come, without preliminaries, to the heart of the matter.

Some complain that in certain historical novels or in certain parts of a historical novel, fact is not clearly distinguished from invention and that, as a result, these works fail to achieve one of their principal purposes, which is to give a faithful representation of history.

In order to show how right these critics may be, I will have to expand upon what they actually say—but without adding anything that isn't already implicit in their own words. And I think if I have them speak this way to the patient, or rather to the author, I will be doing nothing more than developing the logical grounds of their complaint:

"The aim of your work was to put before me, in a new and special form, a richer, more varied, more complete history than that found in works which more commonly go by this name, as if by *antonomasia*. The history we expect from you is not a chronological account of mere political and military events or, occasionally, some other kind of extraordinary happening; but a more general representation of the human condition, in a time and place naturally more circumscribed than that in which works of history, in the more usual sense of the word, ordinarily unfold. In a way, there is the same difference between the usual sort of history and your own as between a geographic map that simply indicates the presence of mountain chains, rivers, cities, towns, and major roads of a vast region and a topographic map, where all of this (and whatever else might be shown in a more restricted area) is presented in greater detail and, indeed, where even minor elevations and less noteworthy particulars—ditches, channels, villages, isolated homes, paths— are clearly marked. Customs, opinions, whether they are generally accepted or peculiar to certain social classes; the private consequences of public events that are more properly called historical, or of the laws or will of the powerful, however these are expressed—in short, all that a given society in a given time could claim as most characteristic of every way of life and of their interactions—this is what you sought to reveal at least as far as you managed, through long hard research, to discover it yourself.[1] And the enjoyment you sought to produce is what naturally comes from acquiring such knowledge, and especially from acquiring it through a representation that I would call living, put into action.

"Granting all this, when has confusing things ever been a means of revealing them? To know is to believe; and for me to believe, when I know what is presented is not all equally true, it is absolutely necessary that I be able to distinguish fact from invention. But how? You want to make real facts known, yet you don't give me the means to recognize them as real? Then why did you want these facts to play an extended, leading role in your work? Why that label "historical" attached to it like a badge and, at the same time, as an attraction? Because you knew very well that there is an interest, as lively and keen as it is singular, in knowing what really happened and how. And after arousing my curiosity and channeling it so, did you think you could satisfy it by presenting me with something that might be reality, but could just as well be a product of your own inventiveness?

"And please don't fail to realize that, in criticizing you this

---

[1] [Ed.] Manzoni's views here may be compared to Balzac's in "L'avertissement du gars" (1828), a text that remained unedited for some time. Here Balzac explains that he wanted the historical novel to present tableaux in which history "would be painted to render perceptible and familiar to all the aftereffects that entire populations experienced from the dissension of royalty, from the disputes of the nobles, or from the revenge of the populace; to offer the results of legal institutions set up for the profit of particular interests, ephemeral needs" (*Les chouans*, [Paris: Garnier, 1957] appendix, p. 423). See the edition by René Guise in *Les fiancés; L'histoire de la colonne infâme; Du roman historique* (Paris: Delta, 1968), hereafter cited as Guise.

way, I also mean to compliment you: I assume I am speaking to a writer who knows how to choose his subjects well and also how to handle them well. If your novel were tedious, filled with ordinary events, possible at any time and therefore not peculiar to any, I would have closed the book without a second thought. But precisely because the event, the character, the circumstances, the means, the consequences that you present attract and hold my attention, a thirst grows in me that is even more keen, insatiable, and, in fact, more reasonable—to know whether I ought to see there a real expression of humanity, nature, Providence, or only a possibility happily found by you. If someone with a reputation for telling tall tales gives you an interesting piece of news, do you say that you "know" that information? Are you left satisfied? Now you (as a novelist, I mean) are like him, like someone who recounts falsehood as readily as truth; and if you do not help me distinguish one from the other, you leave me as dissatisfied as he does.

"Instruction and delight were your two purposes; but they are so bound together that when you fail to achieve one, the other escapes you as well: your reader does not feel delighted, precisely because he does not feel instructed."

Surely these critics could state the case better; but even when they state it this way, one must confess they are right.

However, as I said at the outset, there are other critics who would like just the opposite. They complain instead that in a given historical novel or in given parts of a historical novel, the author does plainly distinguish factual truth from invention; this, they say, destroys the unity that is the vital condition of this or any other work of art. Let us try to see in a bit more detail the basis for this second complaint.

"What," I believe they mean to ask, "is the essential form of the historical novel? The story. And what can one imagine that is more opposed to the unity, to the continuity of the story's effect, to the connection, to the collaboration, to the *coniurat amice* [the friendly league] [2] of each part in producing a total impression, than presenting some of these parts as true and others as the product of invention? The latter, shaped properly, will be just like the former

---

[2] Horace *Ars poetica* 411.

except that they are not true, except that they lack the special ineffable quality of something real. Now, if you point out the quality of truth in those parts that possess it, you deprive your story of its only reason for being, replacing the commonality of its various parts with something that underscores their inconsistency, even their antagonism. By telling me in so many words, or letting me know in some other way, that something is a fact, you force me—whether this was your purpose or not is irrelevant—to think that what preceded it was not fact and that what follows will not be fact either; that the former deserves the credence we lend to positive truth, while the latter deserves only that very different sort of belief that we give to the verisimilar. You naturally lead me to think that the narrative form, though applied to both truth and invention, is really proper and natural only to the former, and merely conventional and factitious for the latter, which amounts to saying that the form is contradictory as a whole.

"And the contradiction could not be more peculiar. You yourself must consider this unity, this homogeneity of the whole extremely important, since you do all you can to achieve it. Choosing from both the real and the possible those elements that harmonize best, you do your utmost to earn the honor that Horace gives to the author of the *Odyssey:*

> And he lies thus, closely mixing the true with the false, so that the middle always refers to the beginning, the beginning to the end.[3]

And for what purpose, if not to lead your readers—seduced, carried away by art—to accept the two parts as a single entity, if you will, just as they are presented? Yet you proceed to undo your own accomplishment, separating on the level of substance that which you have joined together in form! Thus you yourself destroy, in the very course of producing it, the illusion that is art's pursuit and reward, and that is so difficult to create and sustain. Don't you see

---

[3] Horace *Ars poetica* 151:
Atque ita mentitur, sic veris falsa remiscet,
Primo ne medium, medio ne descrepet imum.
[Manzoni also notes that the translation cited in his text is from Metastasio.]

that joining together bits of copper and bits of tin does not make a bronze statue?"

How to answer these critics? To tell the truth, they are probably right.

A friend of mine, whom I recall with affection and esteem, used to relate a curious scene he had witnessed at the house of a justice of the peace in Milan, many years ago. He had found the judge between two litigants, one of whom was hotly pressing his case; and when he had finished, the judge said to him, "You are right." "But, your honor," the other said quickly, "you must hear me too before deciding." "That is only proper," replied the judge, "speak up and I will listen." The second man then presented his case so effectively, and was so successful, that the judge said to him, "You are right too." At that point, one of the judge's children of seven or eight years who, though quietly playing at his side with some kind of toy, had been listening to the debate, raised his astonished little face and exclaimed, not without a certain air of authority: "But daddy! It's not possible for both to be right." "Well, you are right too," said the judge. How it all ended, either my friend did not report or I have forgotten, but evidently the judge reconciled all his reactions, by showing Tom as well as Harry that, if he was right in one sense, he was wrong in another. I shall try to do the same with my two sets of critics. And I shall do it in part by using the litigants' own arguments—but drawing from them consequences that neither drew.

My response to the first is: When you demand that the author of a historical novel allow you to distinguish what really happened from what he has invented, you certainly have not considered whether this can be done at all. You prescribe the impossible, nothing less. To convince yourself, simply try to imagine for a moment how reality and invention must be melded in order to form a single story. For instance, in order to detail the historical events to which the author has tied his plot—for surely you would grant that historical events should figure in a historical novel—he will have to combine both real circumstances, drawn from history or other sources (what could better help present those events in their true and, if you will, distinctive form?) and verisimilar circumstances of his own invention. After all, you want him to give you, not just the bare bones of history, but something richer, more complete. In a way, you want him to put the flesh back on the skeleton that is history. For the same reasons, he will have historical characters—and surely you are happy to find historical characters in a historical novel—say and do both what they really said and did as flesh and blood, and what the author has imagined them saying or doing as befits their character and those parts of the plot in which he has given them a role.

Reciprocally, he will tend to include in his invented actions both invented circumstances and circumstances taken from real events of that time and place, for what better way is there to create actions that *could* have occurred in a given time and place? In the same way, he will lend his invented characters both ideal words and actions and also words and actions really said and done in that time and place—quite content to make these ideal figures more lifelike by incorporating in them elements of truth. This should be enough to make you see that the author could not possibly make the distinctions that you ask of him. Or, rather, that he could not try to make them without fracturing his narrative—and I do not mean every now and then, but every moment, many times in one page, often within a single sentence—to say: this is real fact, taken from reliable sources; this is my own invention, but patterned on reality; these words were actually said by the character to whom I attribute them, but on a very different occasion, in circumstances that I have not included in my novel; these other words, which I put in the mouth of an imaginary character, were actually spoken by a real person, or, it was common talk, and so on. Would you call a work like that a "novel"? Would you find it worth any name at all? Could an author even conceive of such a work?

Perhaps you will tell me that you never intended to ask so much.[4] And you may be right. But I am seeking to understand what

---

[4] [Ed.] It was, though, what at least some critics contemporary to Manzoni asked. Stendhal, for instance, notes that the historical novel "is distancing itself as much as possible from the romance . . . but in so doing, a thousand shadows are spread over history proper. I believe that in the end, the authorities will be constrained to order these new novelists to choose: either to write pure histories or pure novels, or, at least, to use crochet hooks to separate one from the other, the truth from the falsity." (Reference to Louis Maigron, *Le roman historique à l'époque romantique*, [Paris: Hachette, 1898], p. 32, n. 3, given by Guise.)

your words logically imply, as well as directly express. Whether you would want the author to distinguish what is "real" in many cases, or only in a few, or even in one case alone, why would you want him to do so at all? As a whim? No, certainly not. Rather, for a very good reason and one that you yourself have stated; because reality, when it is not presented in a way that makes it recognizable as such, neither enlightens nor satisfies. And does this reason apply only now and then? Hardly; it is by nature a general concern, equally applicable in all cases. And so, if other readers were to complain of similar discomfort elsewhere in the novel, would their complaints not merit the same consideration as yours? Yes, of course, since they are prompted by the same concern: the demand for reality. You see, once you ask the historical novel to identify reality here or there, you are really asking it to identify reality throughout: an impossibility, as I have shown or, rather, led you to see.

Now here is what I say to my other critics: According to you, distinguishing real fact from invention in a historical novel destroys the homogeneity of its effect, the unity of the reader's belief. But tell me, if you would, how you can destroy what does not exist? Don't you see that this inconsistency resides in the basic elements, you might even say in the raw materials, of the work? When, for example, the Homer of the historical novel injects Prince Edward and his landing in Scotland into *Waverley*,[5] he does nothing to alert you that he is dealing with real persons and real facts. The same can be said when he has Mary Stuart flee from the castle of Lochlevan, Louis XI, king of France, sojourn at Plessiz-les Tours, Richard the Lion-Hearted make his expedition to the Holy Land, and so on.[6] It is the characters and the facts themselves that appear this way; it is they that absolutely demand, and inevitably obtain, that unique, exclusive, and ineffable belief that we give to things taken to be fact. This is a belief that I would call historical, to distinguish it from that other unique, exclusive, and ineffable belief that we lend to things known to be merely verisimilar, and that I call poetic. To tell the truth, the damage had already been done before those charac-

[5] [Ed.] *Homer*: Walter Scott (1771–1832); *Waverley*: the first novel (1814) of Walter Scott and for a long time the most famous.

[6] [Ed.] In *The Abbey* (1820), *Quentin Durward* (1823), and *The Talisman* (1824), respectively.

ters appeared on the scene. For in picking up a "historical novel," the reader knows well enough that he will find there *facta atque infecta*[7]—things that occurred and things that have been invented, two different objects of two different, fully contrary, sorts of belief. How can you accuse the author of such a work of creating disharmony? How can you demand that he maintain throughout his work a unity that its very title has rejected?

You too might say that I exaggerate your claims, that the fact that there are some inevitable difficulties is no reason to add others; that, even if the unified belief we expect from art cannot be had in full, there is no need to diminish it further; that by alerting the reader or by intimating that a given thing is really true, the author creates historical beliefs that perhaps would not otherwise emerge and that are at cross-purposes with art.

Perhaps; but what is the alternative? One of two things, both in my view just as much at cross-purposes with art: deception or doubt.

Perhaps if the reader had not been told that an event in the novel had actually occurred, he would have accepted and enjoyed it as a nice poetic invention. But is this the purpose of art? A fine endeavor, a fine artistic procedure that would consist, not in creating verisimilitude, but in leaving the reader ignorant that what is presented is real! A nice artistic device, one whose effect would depend upon accidental ignorance! For if, while enjoying the apparent poetic invention, the reader were approached and told, "You know, that is an actual fact, taken from a specific document," the poor man would be brought down with a thud from the poetic skies onto the field of history. Art is art to the extent that it produces, not just any effect, but a definitive one. And if this is so, the view that truth alone is beautiful is not only plausible but profound; for the verisimilar (the raw material of art)[8] once offered and accepted as such,

---

[7] "Sacri igitur vates, facta atque infecta canentes. . . ." ["Then the sacred poets, singing the true and also the false. . . ."] (Vida *Poetica* 3.112.)

[8] [Ed.] There is a similarity between Vigny's definitions of art in the preface to *Cinq-Mars* and some of Manzoni's. For instance, Vigny's "truth of fact" corresponds to Manzoni's "positive truth" or "real truth"; and Manzoni's view of the verisimilar seems to be at one with Vigny's "truth of art." The difference, of course, is that for Manzoni the truth of art is not easily reconciled with the truth of fact.

becomes a truth that is altogether different from the real,[9] but one that the mind perceives forever, one whose presence is irrevocable. Though it is an object that might come to be forgotten, it can never be destroyed through disillusionment. A beautiful human figure, conceived by a sculptor, never ceases to be a beautiful specimen of the verisimilar; should the sculpture crumble, so would our chance knowledge of that verisimilar; yet its incorruptible essence would survive. But if at a distance in the twilight someone saw a man standing straight and still on a building among some statues and took the man to be a statue himself, would you call that impression a product of art?

It could also happen that a reader, not told by the author that something particularly drawing his attention is a fact, but suspecting that this might be the case because of the nature or, better, the subject matter of the historical novel, might remain doubtful and hesitate, certainly through no fault of his own, quite against his will. To believe, to believe swiftly, readily, fully, is the wish of every reader, except one who reads to criticize. And we take as much pleasure in believing in the purely verisimilar as in real facts, but— you have said it yourself—with a different, even contrary sort of belief. And still, I might add, one condition must always be met: our mind must be able to identify what is before it in order to lend it the appropriate belief. By concealing the reality in what he tells, the author would, as you might wish, keep the reader from lending it a historical belief, but this at the risk of denying him the chance of any belief. Whatever you may say, this effect also runs counter to the purposes of art; for what is less conducive to the unity and ho-mogeneity of the reader's belief than no belief at all?

It is precisely to prevent both the deception I referred to earlier and this uncertainty, precisely to avoid playing a miserable trick on the reader, and, rather, to respond to a probable wish or tacit question of his, that an author can at times be sorely tempted, almost compelled, to point out reality plainly. It is because he senses how

Vigny finds this far less problematic, since his position gives freer reign to the artist's subjective creation and, therefore, to the truth of art.

[9] See the dialogue that follows this essay. [In the *Opere Varie*, the dialogue is the *Dell'invenzione*.]

much may be lacking in what he writes when it lacks historical support. I am not saying that he is doing the right thing; I don't deny that he does something directly and plainly contrary to the unity of his work: I am saying that to refrain from doing so would not help achieve that unity. He acts like Molière's poor master Jacques[10] who appears first in the cook's jacket, then in the coachman's shirt, because his master, the Miser, wants him to act in both capacities and he has agreed to it.

Summing up all these pros and cons, we can, I think, now conclude that both critics are right: both those who want historical reality always to be represented as such and those who want a narrative to produce in its reader a unified belief. But both are wrong in wanting both effects from the historical novel, when the first effect is incompatible with its form, which is narrative, and the second is incompatible with its materials, which are heterogeneous. Both critics demand things that are reasonable, even indispensable; but they demand them where they cannot be had.

But if this is the case, then I might expect to hear that, in the final analysis, it is the historical novel itself that is completely at fault.

This is precisely my point. I had hoped to show, and I think I have shown, that the historical novel is a work in which the necessary turns out to be impossible, and in which two essential conditions cannot be reconciled, or even one fulfilled. It inevitably calls for a combination that is contrary to its subject matter and a division contrary to its form. Though we know it is a work in which history and fable must figure, we cannot determine or even estimate their proper measure or relation. In short, it is a work impossible to achieve satisfactorily, because its premises are inherently contradictory. Its critics ask too much of it—but too much in what sense? In terms of its potential? Exactly. But here precisely is its critical flaw. Ordinarily, one should be able to ask that factual truth be recognizable as such and that a narrative evoke a homogeneous belief from its reader. But the fact is that in the historical novel the two are at odds, which is unfortunate for the historical novel because the two

---

[10] [Ed.] *Jacques:* cook and coachman for Arpagone in the comedy *The Miser,* by Molière (1622–73).

are precisely meant to go together. And if we needed proof of this, we could readily find it in one of the two modes of writing that the historical novel counterfeits and corrupts, namely, history. For history in fact sets out to tell real facts and so to produce in the reader a unified belief, the credence we lend to positive truth.

But, it may be asked, can we actually get this out of history? Does history really create in its reader a succession of unproblematic and rational beliefs? Or doesn't it often leave the credulous deceived and the more reflective in doubt? Even apart from any will to deceive, has there ever been a history containing nothing but the clear and honest truth?

History, it is true, does not lack its tall tales, even its lies. But these are the historians' fault and are not endemic to the genre. When we say that a historian is embellishing, that he is making a jumble of fact and invention, that we do not know what to believe, we mean to fault him for something he could have avoided. And after all, he did have an alternative, as simple as it was sure. For what could be simpler than refraining from invention? Do you really think the author of a historical novel has this means available to avoid deceiving his reader?

It is just as clear that even the most conscientious, most meticulous historian will not give us, by a long shot, all the truth or as plain a truth as we might wish. But even here it is not the art of history that is to blame; it is its subject matter. For an art to be good and rational, it need not be able to achieve its aim fully and perfectly: no art does. Good and rational art is an art which sets a sensible objective and uses the most suitable means to achieve it, the means that, when applied to the right material, will achieve it as far as the human intellect allows. It is possible to obtain and convey, if not perfect knowledge, then at least a reasonably accurate impression about certain real facts, about the human condition in a given time and place. This is what history tries to do, assuming it is in good hands. It may not go as far as one might wish, but it does not willfully drag its feet. It does not overcome all the obstacles—far from it—but it refrains from creating any. If it leaves you sometimes in doubt, that is only because it itself is in doubt. History even makes use of doubt (when something is on the right track, everything suits its purpose). It not only openly confesses doubt but, when necessary, promotes it, sustains it, and attempts to substitute it for false convictions. History makes you doubt because it intends to have you doubt, quite unlike the historical novel which encourages you to believe while at the same time removing what is necessary to sustain belief. In the doubt provoked by history, the mind comes to rest—if not quite at its goal, at least at the limit of its possibilities. Here, it draws satisfaction, so to speak, from a relatively final act, from the only achievement of which it was capable.

The doubt provoked by the historical novel, on the other hand, is disquieting. The mind sees in the subject matter before it the possibility of a further act, the desire for which has been supplied, but the means for which has at the same time been taken away. I suspect there is no author of historical novels, or even of a single historical novel, who has not been asked once or twice whether a certain character, fact, or circumstance was true or invented by him. I also suspect that the author must have said to himself: "Traitor! Your innocent question veils a lethal criticism: you are basically complaining that my book has left you, or, rather, caused you to tug at the author's sleeve. I am well aware that a book should make you want to know more than it tells, but that is a different matter. What you want to know are things of which I have already spoken. You ask me, not to add, but to unravel."

It might not be out of place to mention that history sometimes also uses the verisimilar, and can do so harmlessly if it uses it properly and presents it as such, thereby distinguishing it from the real. It can do this without impairing the narrative unity, for the simple reason that the verisimilar does not really try to become part of the narrative. It is merely suggested, advanced, considered, in short, not narrated on the same level or melded with real facts as is the case in the historical novel. There isn't even any danger that this will ruin the unity of the work, for what more natural bond or continuity is there than that between knowledge and inference? When the mind becomes aware of information that arouses its interest but that is fragmentary or lacking crucial details, it tends to invoke the ideal. The ideal must bear a similar general relationship of possibility[11]

---

[11] [Ed.] At this point in the original, we witness a rare linguistic event, a Manzonian neologism: *compossibilità*.

with what remains of the real, and also the same particular relationship with it—whether of cause, effect, means, manner, or concomitance—as must have had the real circumstances, whose traces are now gone. It is a characteristic of man's impoverished state that he can know only something of what has been, even in his own little world; and it is an aspect of his nobility and his power that he can conjecture beyond what he can actually know. When history turns to the verisimilar, it does nothing other than favor or promote this tendency. It stops narrating momentarily and uses, instead, inductive reasoning, because ordinary narrative is not the best instrument for this, and in adjusting to a different situation, it adopts a new purpose. In fact, all that is needed to clarify the relationship between fact and verisimilar is that the two appear distinct. History acts almost like someone who, when drawing a city map, adds in a distinctive color the streets, plazas, and buildings planned for the future and who, while distinguishing the potential from the actual, lets us see the logic of the whole. History, at such moments, I would say, abandons narrative, but only in order to produce a better narrative. As much when it conjectures as when it narrates, history points to the real; there lies its unity. Where has the unity of the historical novel gone, or, rather, how can it ever develop a unity while it is wandering between opposing goals?

This question permits me to anticipate another objection, even less well founded, but to be expected since it invariably arises in such discussions. We were talking about the historical novel, so the objection goes, and you are comparing it to history, forgetting that they are two types of work with some similar, but also some completely different, purposes.

Quite clearly, such an objection simply begs the question. Certainly, if the historical novel has an equally logical purpose, but one distinct from that of history, it would be odd to compare it with the purpose and methods of history. But the question is precisely whether the historical novel has a logical and therefore attainable purpose of its own and whether, as a consequence, it can have distinct methods to promote it. The purpose of an art reflects its raw material, that is, its subject matter or, rather, its various subject matters. To understand what is peculiar to a material as handled by one art form is to understand what is peculiar to it as handled by any, actual or potential. Since the historical novel finds one of its sources in the peculiarly historical, it should, to this extent, be compared to history. The fact that one can do nothing with historical truth but represent it plainly as such is not a function of the genre in which it appears; it is a function of historical truth itself. Alchemy too had a purpose of its own, distinct from chemistry's, though of course it remained to be achieved. Alchemy also assumed there was a suitable methodology, if only it could be found. Still, there was no better way to learn about alchemy than to compare its experiments and processes of thought with those of chemistry; both, after all, worked with metals. How strange it would have been to hear, "That is all well and good for chemistry, but this is alchemy."

The historical novel does not have a logical purpose of its own; it counterfeits two, as I have shown. Of course, a recital of its purpose—to represent the human condition in a historical era through invented actions—gives an appearance of unity. But for there to be in fact a rational unity (that is, a correspondence between means and ends), something more is necessary, something that has been gratuitously and falsely assumed. The means, indeed the only means, to represent a human condition (or anything else we want to put into words) is to relate our understanding of it as it has emerged from a variety of facts, certain or probable—with whatever limitations and gaps inhere in them, or, rather, in our present ability to know them. It is, in sum, to share with others the final victorious words that we utter to ourselves when things become clearest. This, of course, is the way one writes history, and by history I refer not merely to a chronological narration of selected human events but to any orderly and systematic account of them. Such is the history to which I propose to compare the historical novel, justifiably, I think, even if a history like this were still only a possibility. In fact, everyone knows that there are many quite good histories of this kind, whose goal is to reveal not so much the political course of a society at a given time as its way of life from any number of points of view.

Perhaps you find that history, particularly of this sort, still falls short of its goal, still fails to exploit what its subject matter, researched and viewed from a broader and more philosophical perspective, has to offer. Perhaps you find that history has neglected certain facts or entire categories of facts whose importance it failed to perceive, or overlooked certain connections or correlations among facts that it had bothered to collect and report, but then left isolated because, at first sight, they seemed to be isolated. Say so then, but say it to history, because history alone can repair the omission. To any writer who sees the chance to deepen our knowledge about this or that historical moment and is willing to take on the task, I say, Bravo! *Macte animo!* [Bless your courage!][12] Search every document from that period that you can find. Even treat as documents writings whose authors never, in their wildest imaginations, dreamt they were writing in support of history. Select, discard, connect, contrast, deduce, and infer. If you do, rest assured that you will arrive at a far more precise, more definitive, more comprehensive, more accurate understanding of that historical moment than there was before. But even so, what do you end up with but conceptions only more firmly implanted?[13]

But suppose this writer were not to deal with his readers just as he deals with himself, were not simply to convey to them the pure unadorned knowledge that his painstaking research has earned him. Suppose instead he were to set it aside, dismantle it privately, and reconstruct it, along with material of a totally different nature, into something bigger and better? Suppose to make it more vital, he were to make it live two different lives and take as a means what before was strictly an end? But the very nature of these materials does not allow them to be enlisted to serve such alien ends. They tend to do promptly their own bidding, not the bidding of others. The resulting compound hardly produces a more complete representation of a real human condition; it does not even produce the incomplete one that a faithful account of the facts would yield. For positive truth exists for the human mind only to the extent that it is known, and it cannot be known unless it can be distinguished from what it is not. In short, trying to represent positive truth by enlarging it with the verisimilar only serves to diminish it, to efface it in part. I have heard an old story, perhaps even true, about a man who

---

[12] [Ed.] The phrase appears in Statius *Thebaid* 7.280, although Manzoni probably had Vergil's words in mind as well: "macte nova virtute, puer; sic itur ad astra" (Vergil *Aeneid* 9.641).

[13] [Ed.] Manzoni uses the word *obbligato*, giving it more or less the meaning it has in music: that is, something that can neither be changed nor omitted.

was more frugal than intelligent, who imagined that he could double the oil for burning by adding to it equal parts of water. He knew enough not to simply pour the water on top of the oil, for surely it would sink to the bottom and the oil would float. But he thought he could, by stirring and beating it well, succeed in making it a homogeneous liquid. He beat and beat, and managed to make of it an awful mess that ran together and filled the oil lamp. But now it was worthless. It was no longer oil; indeed, as far as giving off light was concerned, it was less than nothing. This our friend realized as soon as he tried to light the wick.

I have saved for last the most considerable and inexorable objection to my position: the facts. All these ideas, I can hear myself saying, make for lovely theories; but the facts upset them all. To give one example, it would be difficult to name, from among both modern and ancient works, many read more widely and with greater pleasure and esteem than the historical novels of a certain Walter Scott. Try as you may to prove that these novels ought not succeed, the fact is they do.

This objection is weighty in appearance only, however, for its power depends entirely on a confusion, on calling something definitive that is still subject to change. That those novels please the public, and rightly so, is an undeniable fact, but it may be true of those particular novels without being true of the historical novel in general. That this genre will continue to find favor, and therefore be written, is more a question than a fact. In this respect, as in so many others, truth for one era is no guarantee of truth for all time. All too many, and too well known, are the judgments of one age that have been revised by those of another. And if, in citing these revisions of judgments so often and with such contempt, we risk giving new judgments, the reason is that we naturally find our present-day decisions more mature, more authoritative, more definitive than those that came before. And this is hardly surprising, for they are our own. What allows us to scorn judgments of the past is that we are the future; this is no small matter. What allows us to have confidence in our own judgments is that we are the present; and this is no less a matter.

Among the well-known examples to which I alluded, however, let me single out one that is especially analogous to our subject. There has probably been no greater vogue than that of the historical-heroic-erotic novels—I find it hard to settle on a single name—of Mlle Scudéry[14] and of other less famous precursors and successors of hers, in a country and century no less cultivated than the France of Louis XIV. We might cite Boileau's[15] confession, in his introduction to the dialogue deprecating those novels, that, "being young when they were the rage, [he] had read them, as indeed everyone read them, with great admiration, and held them to be masterpieces of the French language."[16]

Of course, it would be even more an eccentricity than an injustice to treat such works as the equals of Walter Scott's. But, for all that separates the authors and the literary genres, there is, as I have suggested, an analogy, even an important point of identity: both are kinds of novels in which history has a role. And let it not be said that those earlier novels only make a pretense of invoking history, almost as a joke, or that no one would possibly think of history in reading those strange sequences of mad and platonic loves or the even stranger speeches and quarrels about them. For how strange it would have seemed to the otherwise quite tolerant readers of *Clélia,* which after all was once very popular and is still even occasionally remembered, had Mlle Scudéry given the name of Virginia to the woman assaulted by Sextus Tarquinius,[17] or made Porsena[18] a king of Macedonia or even of Cisalpine Gaul, or had had Clélia throw herself into the Euphrates or even the Po to swim away from the enemy camp.[19] These earlier readers were not utterly indifferent to the truthfulness of the history that entered into such

---

[14][ed.] Madeleine de Scudéry (1607–1701), author of novels such as *Artamèna; ou, Le grand Cyrus* and *Clélie,* both of which were popular in their day, both in France and abroad.

[15][Ed.] Nicolas Boileau-Despréaux (1636–1711), author of *L'art Poétique* and the figurehead of literary classicism.

[16]"Les héros de roman," dialogue. The essay was written many years later, and for a new edition.

[17][Ed.] It is Lucretia who was dishonored by Sextus Tarquinius (Livy *Roman History,* 1.62–3).

[18][Ed.] Livy also recalls that Porsena was a king of Etruria, who made war on Rome (*Roman History* 2.9).

[19][Ed.] An allusion to a famous episode in Mlle de Scudéry's novel: Clélia, a young Roman, given as a hostage to Porsena, saves herself by swimming across the Tiber in the midst of a shower of arrows.

works; they were only much more tolerant than present-day readers would be. They did pay attention to history when they read these novels, and why not? After all, if the public accepted and enjoyed works in which history played a vital part and supplied the basics of plot and character as well as time and place, we can only conclude that it wanted history to be there. And the public could scarcely want history to be there without paying attention to it. Still, it must be admitted that readers then paid less attention to it than present-day readers do.

Now, did this change come about suddenly, all at once? It was not at all like that, nor could it have been. The public's tolerance diminished gradually. It demanded ever more history and, with it, ever greater historical detail. This was so not only with the ephemeral and rather silly kind of composition I have been referring to but with all works consisting of history and invention. I am not talking about a steady, continuous process, about a uniform trend; but, beyond the temporary halts and random backward steps that always take place in the development of ideas and events, this was the overall direction, the dominant course. As the tolerance of the public declined—partly as a result of this and partly aside from it, but always because of the same underlying desire for historical truth— writers grew less bold. To an extent, the public (in which professional critics naturally figure prominently) demonstrated, whether by criticism or simple neglect, that it would no longer tolerate extreme alterations of history, thereby forcing writers to include more actual history and greater historical detail. To an extent, the writers themselves, whether by reflecting on their art in the abstract or simply sensing more keenly than ever the critical importance of historical truth in the practice of writing, found new ways to give it prominence in their works. For a while, as always happens with solutions to problems that at the time seem momentous, each of these theoretical or practical responses seemed adequate. But then the demand for historical truth that, for reasons both independent of art and within art itself, continued to grow in the process just described, led to still newer needs and a search for still newer solutions. Each successive solution was a fact, none *the* fact. Each adjustment was progress; none was, or could have been, the destination. For nothing (and we always return to this point) can be the final destination on the path of historical truth but, relatively speaking of course, total and pure historical truth. When parts are alike, improving one strengthens the whole; when they are not alike, improving one destroys it.

With this, I am ready to make explicit what is implied in all I have said up to now, namely, that the historical novel is hardly unique in the inherent contradiction of its premises and in its resulting inability to take on a convincing and stable form. I would not join those who have called it or now call it a false and spurious genre. To me, this view rests upon the entirely erroneous assumption that the way had been found to combine history and invention and that it had worked, but the historical novel came along and ruined it. The fact is the historical novel is not a false genre, but a species of a false genre which includes all compositions that try to mix history and invention, whatever their form. Being the most modern such species, the historical novel is only the most refined and ingenious effort yet to meet the challenge, as if the challenge could ever be met.

No one, I think, would deny that rendering a final judgment on the historical novel required an inquiry of this kind, though I very much doubt that my view will quickly win favor. Let me try to strengthen it, by turning from the premises of the historical novel to those of the epic and tragedy, two other important and well-known forms of the genre, and comparing the changes that occurred in them, both in theory and practice, in their relationship to history. These changes (as if we did not know or could ever forget it) are marked by glorious monuments of genius, monuments that last precisely because genius has a way of perpetuating even things that by their nature are not otherwise certain to last. Still, these variations must themselves stem from a mighty force, for even the beauty and majesty alive in those literary monuments could not halt its movement. Molded by masterful hands, but also by instruments that are no longer apt, these monuments say, in effect, to those who look at them long and carefully enough: admire me, but do otherwise.

PART II

The purpose of the epic as generally understood is to portray a great and celebrated event, while broadly inventing its causes, means, complications, manner, and circumstances, all with a view to giving the reader greater enjoyment and inspiration than a simple and straightforward historical narrative would allow.

I readily admit that to propose this under present circumstances, simply as something that might be done, as if for the first time, a priori, and without any concrete illustration, would strike the tutored and untutored alike as strange indeed. A reader lacking detailed knowledge of a great and celebrated event, and whose familiarity with it is confined to the more or less abstract formula that has become shorthand for it, would never understand why an author should ask him to consider that event unless it were precisely to relate its causes, means, complications, manner, and circumstances and, in so doing, remedy his meager and only very general conception of it. A reader with more extensive and detailed knowledge would find the enterprise even more bizarre, to say the least. Why detach the event from any part, much less the better part, of the historical circumstances with which it is naturally bound up and interwoven, and attach it instead to imaginary ones? Though ready, of course, to accept whatever might add to or improve his understanding, this reader would be equally ready to reject whatever might adulterate it, reacting with the "incredulus odi" that is appropriate not only to the particular kind of falsehood to which Horace applied these words,[1] but to any falsehood of whatever kind or degree that seeks to displace the truth.

[1] Horace *Ars poetica* 185–88:
Nec pueros coram populo Medea trucidet,

It is easy, in fact, to see why historians, particularly modern ones, seek to promote this attitude: they know their own best interest and strive, as much as any epic poet, to produce both enjoyment and inspiration. This is why they emphasize how little was known previously of the real circumstances of the event or series of events they are about to describe, great or small (and so much the better if great), and to what length they had to go to rid the material of all that had been imposed upon it by the bad faith of some or the imagination of others. Historians promise that readers will find in their works information about primary and secondary causes, about customs and circumstances, that is every bit as new and unexpected as it is true—in short, that it is only due to their research and observation that a more ordered, comprehensive, and straightforward conception of events can be had than the rather false and confused idea that was possible before.[2] It would be unthinkable to propose to readers and writers who share this sort of understanding that they distort their conceptions of important events to make them the subject and theme of a new sort of work! The proposal, to elaborate just a little, would practically amount to this:

Some memorable events of the past may be called great both on account of their causes and their effects. They are great in the first respect because of the extraordinary concurrence of human plans and actions that worked, even in their conflict, to make events turn out as we know them. They are great in the second because of the extraordinary changes in social conditions that they produced. Besides its primary causes, of course, each event has a number of secondary causes that enter at different points in its de-

---

aut humana palam coquat exta nefarius Atreus,
aut in avem Progne vertatur, Cadmus in anguem.
Quodcumque ostendis mihi sic, incredulus odi
[So Medea ought not slay her boys before the
audience, nor should Atreus cook his horrid banquet of
human flesh, nor Procne be turned into a bird,
Cadmus into a snake. Anything that you thus
put before my eyes I discredit and abhor.]

[2] [Ed.] Manzoni, when writing as a historian, often promised his readers something of the sort. See, for instance, the note that accompanies *Il conte di Carmagnola*, the first paragraph of the *Discorso sopra alcuni punti della storia longobardica*, and even the beginning of chapter 31 of *I promessi sposi*.

velopment. Each event encountered both resistance and support, underwent both delays and advances, and had both its chance and its special or, so to speak, peculiar characteristics. The historian surely performs a meaningful and useful service when he gathers all this information, when he sorts it out, when he identifies for each thing and each person its particular characteristics and contribution to the whole, and when he studies and establishes the actual sequence of events—all of this so that the reader may, while appreciating the significance and the uniqueness of the result, at the same time find it both very natural and even quite inevitable.

Yet there is something else and, in a certain sense, something better to do, namely, to represent those events as they ought to have been, so as to heighten still further the enjoyment and inspiration they produce. This is the part of the poet. It is up to you to make a fresh choice among the aspects of the event, to omit those that do not serve your own more lofty purpose, and to adapt as you find best those that do. It is up to you to imagine the sort of difficulties that likely delayed or diverted the course of events, as well as the forces it probably took to overcome them. It is up to you to conceive of the chance happenings, plans, passions, and, to portray all of these more easily, the characters that probably played a role of some importance. It is up to you to trace the path that events might have taken to arrive where they did.

As I have said, to propose a project like this in an a priori fashion today would seem strange. It is probably no exaggeration to say that it would not occur to anyone to do so.

In fact, if we look a bit further, or simply reflect on what we know, we will find that this never happened. The literary epic—of which the historical epic was not even the first type—did not come into the world, so to speak, in a planned fashion. It was not the realization of an abstract prior concept. Quite the contrary. The primitive, or what might be called the spontaneous, epic was nothing other than history, which for present purposes means whatever was accepted as history by those to whom it was told or sung. Two outstanding monuments of that history still remain: the *Iliad* and the *Odyssey*. Even after these could no longer be accepted as true and authentic history, they remained a source of immense pleasure on other grounds and thus could be appreciated from a purely aesthetic point of view. From this, the idea naturally arose of composing other works based upon the same idea and, since even imitation does not move by leaps, also of using themes similarly drawn from the traditions of the age of fables. Such was the earliest form of the literary epic. It differed from the original spontaneous epic in that it had neither the effect nor the purpose of creating belief in what it told. But it did retain the important quality of recounting things for which there were no positive and verifiable historical counterparts. This was no longer history, but at the same time there was no longer a history with which it had to contend. Once it ceased to pass for truth, the verisimilar could freely display and use its own magnificent power. No longer did it compete on the same terrain with positive truth, which, like it or not, also has a distinct purpose and a characteristic force that works independently of all contrary conventions. Of this form, the most splendid remaining monument is the *Aeneid*.

We could infer that the Homeric poems were originally accepted as history, even if there were no other evidence to this effect, simply from knowing that no other history was then available and that peoples do not remain long without it. They want to know the truth, and a lot of it, about the conduct of human beings, especially their ancestors, quite without supposing that they might derive some other kind of pleasure from contemplating the merely verisimilar. Later came the enlargement and transformation of traditions through the gradual and measured resort to imagination for details that memory could no longer supply. It doubtless was an easy, spontaneous and, in part, almost involuntary invention of its authors, and one that the public was quite ready to accept. It is certainly not the least thoughtful or knowledgeable who have hypothesized that these poems may not have been written by a single author, then scattered, if you will, by those who sang them to the public more or less faithfully, and finally later reconstructed. Rather, so the theory goes, these works are a collection, a splicing together of successive efforts around the same themes, and their true author is "Homer absorbed into the crowd of people," as Vico[3] says with his typically bold and even more typically sound

---

[3] Giambattista Vico, *Scienza nuova*, book 3; *Discoverto del vero Omero*.

originality. Such histories, in any case, were judged by their credibility, not by "good taste," which had not yet been born. Just imagine how the rhapsodes would have fared had they said, and been able to say, "Good people, we could have told you the events of which we shall sing as they really occurred, so far as we can tell, but to provide you better entertainment, we have decided to present them differently, artificially, adding and subtracting as art dictates."

The romances of the Middle Ages, sung by a new variety of rhapsodes known as troubadours, giullari, and minstrels exemplify the strict regard for truth of a story-loving public. Out of these romances evolved a new epic that took from them the name "romantic." Here are some words on this subject from the scholar La Curne de Sainte-Palaye:[4]

> Originally, it seems, the only subject of those poems was history, if we can use the word history for tales composed in meter and rhyme to make them easier to remember. . . .
>
> The chronicles of San Dionigi were held in such high esteem in the thirteenth and fourteenth centuries that historians found that relying on their authority was an unsurpassed way of gaining the confidence of their readers.[5]

Let me quote, from among the passages of the historical poets cited by the learned critic, one by a Philippe Mouskes, who was writing at the beginning of the thirteenth century. This is how he responds to the charge of not having been careful enough in selecting his authors:

> . . . Quant un me conseilla
> que trop obscurement savoie
> les faiz que je ramentevoie,
> et que s'a Saint Denis allasse,
> le voir des Gestes y trouvasse,
> non pas menconges ne frivoles;

---

[4][Ed.] Jean-Baptiste de La Curne de Sainte-Palaye (1697–1781) studied ancient chronicles and works of the troubadours. His writings include the *Glossaire de l'ancienne langue française* and a *Dictionnaire des antiquités françaises* (40 vols.).

[5]La Curne de Sainte-Palaye, *Mémoires de l'Académie des Inscriptions et Belles-Lettres* 15:580.

bientost après cestes paroles
m'en vins là, et tant esploitai,
que veu ce que je convoitai,
lors alai faus apercevant
quanque j'avoie fait devant;
Si l'ardit c'on ni deust croire,
et me pris à la vraie histoire,
jouste la quele je mesis? [6]

Considering that they actually consulted these famous chronicles, what did they find in them?

Come cils Kalles la conquist toute entièrement en son tens, et
la fist obaïr à ses commandemens;
    Come Fernagus un Jaianz du lignage Goulie estoit venu à la
cité de Nadres des contrées de Surie: si l'avoit envoié l'amiraus
de Babilone contre Kallemaine pour deffendre la terre d'Es-
paigne:
    Comment Rollans occist le Roi Marsile, et puis comment il
fendit le perron, quant il cuida despiecer s'espée; et puis comment il sonna derechief l'oliphant, que Kalles oï de VIII miles
loing. [7]

---

[6] [Ed.] René Guise (in *Les fiancés; L'histoire de la colonne infâme; Du roman
historique* [Paris: Delta, 1968], hereafter cited as Guise) notes that Manzoni here has
mistakenly attributed the poem to Philippe Mouskes. It is in fact the work of
Guillaume Guiart. In English, the text reads as follows:

> When they told me that I was too confused about the facts I recorded and that,
> if I went to Saint Denis I would find the truth about these deeds, and not lies or
> frivolousness, I went there at once. I searched so hard that, having learned
> what I ardently desired and discovered that all I had done was false, I burnt my
> past work so no one would believe it and I followed the true story closely, in
> accordance with which I set it down on paper.

In the original edition, Manzoni supplies a few words in Italian to help his readers
translate: "il vero" for "le voir," "bruciai" for "l'ardit," and "messi in carta" for "je
mesis."

[7] *Chroniques de Saint Denis: Gestes le grant roi Kallemaine, Recueil des histo-
riens des Gaules et de la France,* vol. 5:

> [How Charlemagne conquered all of Spain entirely in his time, and made it
> obey his commands; how Fernagus, a giant of Goliath's lineage, had come to
> the city of Nadres from the country of Soria, where the admiral of Babylon
> had sent him against Charlemagne to defend Spanish lands. In what way Ro-

To La Curne's remark might profitably be added a similar one, based on the vastly greater research of my famous departed friend, Fauriel:[8]

> Authors of romantic epics of the Carolingian cycle invariably hold themselves out as true historians. They always begin by proclaiming that they will tell nothing but what is true and authentic. They always cite documents, that is, authorities to which one points in order to convince. Ordinarily, these will be precious chronicles, preserved in one monastery or other, to which the author has had the fortune to be led with the help of some learned monk. . . .
>
> The way they describe their stories only underscores their claim to have drawn them from venerable sources. They use expressions like "songs of old history," "of high history," "of heroic exploits," "of great baronies," and they do so not to boast. Literary vanity is of no consequence to them compared with the wish to be believed or to pass for simple translators, for mere conveyors of legends or sacred histories.[9]

Those protests serve the same function as the Homeric invocation to the goddess of memory. They show that, even at a time when history was being written, it was the wish to believe that made the epic tale attractive to the least informed part of the population, that is, to the part that most closely resembled the entire population in the age of Homer, or of the Homers, if you prefer.

Proceeding with this brief outline of classical antiquity, it is clear that even in Rome the epic first appeared clothed with the authority of history.[10] (Fortunately, our subject does not call for com-

---

land had killed King Marsilio, and then how he broke the rock, when he wanted to break his sword; and then how he sounded the horn again that Charlemagne heard eight miles away.]
Again, Manzoni supplies some Italian words and phrases to help his reader: "Carlomagno" for "cils Kalles"; "la Spagna" for "toute"; "il masso" for "le perron"; "il corno" for "l'oliphant."]

[8][Ed.] Claude Fauriel, 1772–1844. See Introduction for Manzoni's friendship with Fauriel.

[9]Fauriel, *Histoire de la poésie provençale*, chap. 25, vol. 2, pp. 281–82.

[10][Ed.] See Vico, *Scienza nuova*.

parable treatment of other antiquities since, though they would be very interesting, they had little to do with the birth of the historical epic.) By the time of Titus Livy, it was already recognized that the story of the founding of Rome was largely a poetic creation.[11] Modern writers have argued, with varying cogency, that this realization occurred even before. The earliest form in which that story came down to us was strictly as history, and it appears that it was only a short time, if ever at all, in the hands of the cyclic poets. This original form was, as Vico said of ancient Roman law, "a serious poem"[12] This seems right, for it is unlikely that the patricians—the consummate keepers, preservers, and consecrators—would have left the story of the founding of those institutions by which they maintained their power over the plebes in the hands of entertainers and masters of the plebes.

The subject of this epic was not a chance and passing federation of princes to destroy a city and return in triumph to their respective states (poor states!), only to find themselves, in the immediate wake of their great victory, quarreling with one another. The subject was the founding and growth of the city (and what a city!) of those patricians themselves. Exactly what Minerva said to Pandarus to induce him to strike Menelaeus, or Iris to Archilles to send him to save the body of Patroclus from the Trojans,[13] made little difference, even to the Greeks. But it would have made an enormous difference if the whims of the popular poets had tampered with the discussions between Numa and Egeria, out of which grew the institutions of the priesthood, the sacred rituals, and the science of augury that remained arcane for so long a time.[14] It was the story of the augur Attus Navius, who miraculously defended his science against the effort of Tarquinius Priscus to establish new tribes without first consulting the oracle, that furnished the basis and sus-

---

[11] "Quae ante conditam, condendamve urbem, poeticis magis fabulis, quam incorruptis rerum gestarum monumentis traduntur, ea nec affirmare, nec refellere in animo est." ["As to what happened before the founding of the City, as to those traditions more suited to poetic creation than to the authentic records of the historian, I have no intention either to affirm or to refute."] (Titus Livy *History of Rome*, preface.)

[12] *Scienza nuova*, book 4, corollary.

[13] *Iliad*, bks. 4, 18.

[14] Livy *History* 1.21–22.

tained the system of augurs and omens which was to govern the making of virtually all decisions [15] and which was the special symbol and province of the patricians.[16] For different stories on such a subject to have been invented—whether by whim or by design— and for them to have been sung to the plebes would have been not only useless but dangerous, for it was against the plebes that the auspices were most often used, and it was the plebes whose actions and free speech they most controlled and abridged, even after such action and speech had been legalized.

A woman figured prominently in the Greek as well as the Latin epic, in the former as cause of a great event, in the latter as cause of a great change. Yet poets could safely expand and embellish the story of Helen, the wife of one of many kings. Even if in Sparta they had agreed to put her story into a single, orthodox form, they could hardly have silenced the poetic gossip of the rest of Greece. On the other hand, Lucrezia [17]—matron, wife of a Roman patrician (the patricians being numerous but always the dominant class)—was the victim who sanctified the passing of the royal aristocracy into the purer aristocracy of consuls. This was no memory to leave to the fertile whims of fantasy.

When, very much later, history returned to the hands of poets, it was to poets of a completely different sort, that is, "literary" poets. By then history had already assumed such a distinct and stable form that scarcely anyone could conceive of making it something of his own. History was still too authoritative for any part to be detached from it and embellished with new stories of any single person's own invention. This explains, if I am not mistaken, why when Ennius wanted to make this history become poetry once again, he could find no better way than to put the whole thing, just

[15] "Ut nihil belli domique postea nisi auspicato gereretur." ["In war as in peace, nothing from now on is done without the auspices being taken."] (Livy *History* 1.36.)

[16] "[Interroganti tribuno 'cur plebeium consulem fieri non oportet,' ut fortasse vere, sic parum utiliter in praesens certamen] respondit, 'quod nemo plebeius auspicia haberet." ["The tribune having asked why a plebeian could not become consul, received this response, perhaps a just one, but surely rather tactless in a discussion such as this, 'because no plebeian can take the auspices.'"] (Livy *History* 4.6.)

[17] [Ed.] Lucrezia, the wife of Collatinus, killed herself after being dishonored by Sextus Tarquinius.

as it stood, into verse.[18] And, judging from the fragments that remain of his *Annals,* once he had taken this path, he naturally went on to bring the history up to date, almost up to his own time. In fact, the title alone (*Annals*) is adequate evidence that Ennius did not conceive the subject of the work to be the "single and complete action, with beginning, middle, and end" that Aristotle, and nearly everyone else, considers the essential quality of the epic poem.[19] Ennius can be regarded, therefore, neither as continuing the Homeric epic nor as founding the historical epic. While the latter shares the former's purpose of representing a single complete action, it differs profoundly by drawing its subject matter from material as different as history is from fable.

The literary and artistic epic, which had been created in imitation of the primitive and spontaneous epic—and how else could it have been created?—first tried to follow that epic and compete with it in the field of fable, before accomplishing its radical transformation. Indeed, a middle stage intervened between the *Iliad* and the *Pharsalia.*[20] But a very special subject, like that of the *Aeneid,* and a very special author, like Vergil, were necessary for art to overcome all the problems involved in imitating something that had come about spontaneously and whose very reason for being was tied to circumstances and a state of mind that no longer existed. Thus there could emerge an original work in a different mode, a work that, while most unlike its archetype, was in no way inferior.

[18] [Ed.] Quintus Ennius, a Latin poet (240–169 B.C.). He composed a lengthy epic entitled the *Annals,* describing all of Roman history from the loves of Mars to his own epoch.

[19] "De narrativa autem, et in metro imitatrice, quod oportet fabulas, quemadmodum in tragediis, constituere dramaticas, et circa unam actionem totam et perfectam, habentem principium et medium et finem." ["As to that poetic imitation which is narrative in form and employs a single meter, the plot surely ought, as in tragedy, to be built on dramatic principles. It should have for its subject a single action, whole and complete, with a beginning, a middle, and an end."] (Aristotle *Poetics,* chap. 22.)

[Ed.] Manzoni notes that for the convenience of those who cannot understand the Greek text, he quotes and will quote elsewhere, when necessary, Vettori's Latin translation, known for being extremely literal. He then adds the words that Dido used to welcome Aeneas and his companions, "Non ignara mali, miseris succurrere disco ("Not ignorant of trouble myself, I have learned to help the distressed.") (Vergil *Aeneid* 1.630.)

[20] [Ed.] See n. 29 below.

Since the story was mythological and yet related to the founding of Rome, it afforded the poet both great artistic freedom and a
subject with the lively interest of history. For one thing, it allowed
him to conjure fantastic visions, *speciosa miracula*,[21] out of that
vast and airy mist of the heroic ages and freely to add his own inventions to existing tales that were at least as well known as history,
but by their very nature invited elaboration. Knowledge of history
and of historical beliefs associated with those times was the science
of an erudite few, and I certainly do not mean to suggest that the
epic of the Augustan age could maintain the same free and easy gait
of the earliest epics. But think how weak and loose its fetters must
have been, in comparison with those that later confined the historical epic. Unlike others who thought they were imitating him, Vergil
did not have to force the gods into events, when the concept of
those events was already fully implanted in the readers' minds without the gods having an active part. He found the gods in the subject
matter itself.[22] It was not Vergil who made his hero the son of a goddess in order to aggrandize him. Nor was it Vergil who, for the first
time, had the goddess go down into battle to help the wounded
hero.[23] The intervention of the other deities either for or against Aeneas followed a conflict already begun, allegiances already pledged.

Yet the theme that had become a virtual sequel to the *Iliad*
was, or rather became, in Vergil's hands, the most monumental and
stirringly patriotic work for the people in whose language it was
written. For Rome was always the real and true subject behind all
these poetic adventures; I would almost call Rome the ultimate subject of the poem. It is for Rome that Olympus is moved and fate
stands still. No matter what the subject, if it was taken from the
history of Rome, it could be neither completely poetic—doubtless a
great disappointment to Vergil—nor more than just one episode
from the city's immense history. It could be nothing more than a
single action caused by prior ones and precipitating still others,

[21] Horace *Ars poetica* 144.

[22] [Ed.] Voltaire writes in his *Essai sur la poésie épique*, a text Manzoni surely
read: "He could not avoid putting Homer's gods on the scene, gods who were almost
his own and who, according to tradition, had themselves guided Aeneas into Italy"
(chapter 3, "Virgile"), cited by Guise.

[23] *Aeneid*, bk. 12; *Iliad*, bk. 5.

a victory making way for other wars, an expansion of the empire only bringing it nearer other peoples to conquer. In the *Aeneid,* Rome may be seen at a distance, but it is seen completely. Leave it to the poet, ever discreet, ever amazing, to keep your eyes gazing in that direction. Leave it to him to portray even its future history, in some cases by quick, masterful allusions to a few particulars, elsewhere more extensively, through splendid poetic inventions like the prophecy of Anchises or the arms of Vulcan. It makes little difference whether inventions are old or new, as long as they have passed through the hands of Vergil.

The reason is that Vergil's poetic style is simply unsurpassed in power. By poetic style, I mean the style that distinguishes itself from common usage by its advantage—and a very important one for anyone who exploits it—in expressing ideas that common usage is not called upon to express, but that still deserve to be expressed once they have been conceived. For even quite ordinary things have qualities and relationships that are more arcane and less well known (if they are known at all) than those that are most closely and commonly associated with them. It is precisely these that the poet seeks to convey and that require of him new locutions. *He speaks almost another language,*[24] because he has such different things to say. And just when he is most transported by emotion or inspiration, just at the threshold, so to speak, of an idea for which common usage has no expression, he finds the special language that captures it and renders it clear to the mind's eye. (Whatever ideas he may have had just before or just after, he certainly cannot think of them now.)

Rarely does he do this, and even more rarely with much success, by inventing new words as scientists do. Almost invariably, it is by combining usual words in unusual ways, since, after all, the special character of poetry is not so much to teach something new as to reveal new aspects of something already known, and the most natural way to do that is to put words with established meaning into new relationships. These formulas seldom pass into common usage, since, as we have said, common usage rarely has occasion to

---

[24] "Poetas quasi alias quadam lingua locutos non conor attingere," (Antonius in Cicero *De oratore* 2.14).

express such ideas and since poetic language is designed to embody intuitions, rather than provide instruments for discourse. Still, when expressions are both true and unusual, as these should be, they are doubly pleasing. What is more, they effectively increase our knowledge, although some would have us believe that all knowable things fall within a small number of categories.[25]

To define poetry is to identify what Vergil did so well. For, more than any other poet, Vergil—with his vital yet controlled imagining of subjects, his intuitions that would shift between the quick and the deliberate precisely because they were so alive, and his genuine feeling for the emotions he invoked—created and filled the need for new, poetically true, and even exotic expressions.[26] And by this I mean a real need, for there was no one less willing than Vergil to innovate if ordinary usage could adequately express his ideas. But frequently it could not, and that is why we so frequently, but not too frequently, come upon those verbal combinations that may surprise but never seem to jar. We might aptly say that this resembles Horace's *callida iunctura*,[27] except that Vergil deserves an even more noble and lofty description. Probably no better words could be found than Vergil's own in describing one use of his art:

[25] No reader, I hope, will confuse the poetic style I refer to here, which is characteristic of every writer, with that silly thing that is improperly called poetic language (an impropriety, for that matter, not peculiar to this case): as if in one language there could be several. It has been made to consist of a certain number of locutions to be used exclusively in verse, like "kingdom of shadows," "melodious swans," "crystal liquids," "consuming time," "flowering season," and similar. These are, for the most part, more or less successful mythological locutions that, once discovered by one poet, others had only to adopt; thus they are at the same time both foreign to common discourse and trivial.

[26] Donatus tells us in the *Life of Vergil* that Vergil, when asked by Maecenas what there would never be too much of, responded that all things, either by quantity or by their resemblance to one another, can eventually become boring, without intending to, except understanding: *Praeter intelligere*. That is the opinion of a philosopher, but it is also the opinion of a poet like Vergil; and it was not the grammarians who were able to suggest it to him.

[27] Horace *Ars poetica* 47–48:
Dixeris egregie, notum si callida verbum
reddiderit iunctura novum.
["You will write with distinction if a skillful
setting makes a well-known word new."]

Nec sum animi dubius verbis ea vincere magnum
Quam sit, et angustis hunc addere rebus honorem;

And he adds:

Sed me Parnassi deserta per ardua dulcis
Raptat amor: iuvat ire iugis qua nulla priorum
Castaliam molli devertitur orbita clivo.[28]

This means: "But I feel I am Vergil." It is tempting to assume that no poem with a style like his could ever fail to appeal, regardless of its subject or its structure. But I know that this cannot be so, for the very fine and careful judgment that guided Vergil in his choice of language must have steered him from any subject, whether of his own creation or borrowed from others, that was not perfectly suited for his art or that lacked intrinsic worth.

Lucan,[29] whom one can call the founder of the historical epic, followed shortly after Vergil. He was, I believe, the first to take as the subject of a long poem a complex event from historic times, whose unity of action stems from the fact that its various parts are linked to one another and lead to a single conclusion. I have chosen to say an event "from historic times," rather than a "historic event," because here lies the real difference between the *Pharsalia* and previous epics, a difference whose importance has not been fully appreciated by critics whose perception of real but secondary differences has tended to obscure the primary and fundamental innovation on which the others depend. The Trojan War, it is true, is more or less a historical fact, like the civil wars of Rome; and the Aeneas who came to Italy after that war can be considered a historical character much like Caesar. For this reason, it might appear that there is no substantial difference between the subjects of the *Iliad* and the *Aeneid,* on the one hand, and the *Pharsalia* on the other, and that Lucan's particular innovations are merely idiosyncratic.

[28] *Georgics* 3.289–93. ["For my part, I know well enough what it is to triumph over my subject with words and how to elevate very slight details by the dignity of verse. But a sweet desire leads me toward the deserted cliffs of Parnassus. I love to walk along those heights, where no wheel has left tracks before me on the gentle slope that leads to Castalia."]

[29] [Ed.] Lucan, author of the *Pharsalia,* tells of the civil war between Pompey and Caesar until the battle of Munda (45 B.C.)

But, unless I am mistaken, even the slightest attention should show that these differences were the natural, if not necessary, consequence of having taken the subject from historic times (that is, from times about which the reader either had or could have had an impression separate and apart from the one the poet used as the basis for his invention). If there was idiosyncrasy, it was that.

Let me mention the two innovations most commonly attributed to Lucan. The first is that he slavishly followed history instead of transforming it freely.[30] But this was because there was history in his subject, and his choice was either to follow it or to contradict it and thereby inevitably run into conflict with an idea already deeply implanted in his readers' minds.[31]

The other innovation is that he excluded the gods from his poetry. But this was because they were not in his subject. And surely to use the parts of one's subject and to introduce extraneous ones are not quite the same thing.

It seems to me that to criticize Lucan for trying to develop, through his plot, a history in verse rather than a poem—other criticisms leveled at the *Pharsalia* are not relevant here—is to fail to consider whether he had any better alternative. Should Lucan instead have chosen a subject from more remote historical times, or

---

[30] [Ed.] Voltaire notes in the *Essai sur la poésie épique* the same two characteristics—and defenses—of Lucan's poetry: "Lucan did not dare to depart from history; through this, he made his poem dry and barren . . . Vergil and Homer had done very well to lead the gods onto the scene; Lucan did just as well to do without them." (Chap. 4, "Lucain.")

[31] Perhaps here one might say that even the *Aeneid* was subject to historical objections and that, for example, the story about Dido was recognized as false ("fabula lascivientis Didonis, quam falsam novit universitas" [Macrobius *Saturnalia* 5.17]) as was the archaic belief on which the poet had based it. I do not deny this flaw, but to my mind it was slight and, above all, not "necessary." This was but a simple, summary concept of the real, a concept almost purely negative, that rose up against a vast and marvelous complex of "verisimilars." Imagine for a moment a similar anachronism (if something contested by chronological data is an anachronism) introduced into a theme from historical (that is, modern) times: what continual and detailed contrasts between fable and history! And I said that the flaw was not necessary in the "fabulous epic" (epic of the marvelous), not because in the historical epic there are such grave, necessary alterations of history, but because there need not be any at all. Moreover, as has been said already—and it is an argument that cuts in our favor—the epic of Vergil could not have all the advantages of the Homeric.

even from the age of fables, so that he would have greater liberty to introduce the gods? Both were attempted with little success, and not by poets of such meager talent that they should largely bear the blame. In fact, had the works of Vergil not survived, these poets would surely be more highly regarded than they are, perhaps even admired; for they had learned from Vergil how to exploit what the Latin language had to offer and, by imitating his use of that language, were able to achieve a more consistently and boldly poetic style than modern languages allow even their most talented writers.

Like Vergil, Silius Italicus[32] gave the gods a part in his poem. But his subject, unlike Vergil's, was the Second Carthaginian War, and his protagonists, Hannibal and Scipio, unlike Aeneas and Turnus, did not have parents in Olympus. They were not "heroes mingling with the gods,"[33] but generals and statesmen of two republics. Imagine the effect even on pagan readers—but readers familiar with Livy and Polybius—when Mars, on entering personally into the battle of Ticino, covers young Scipio with his shield and speaks to him from his airborne chariot,[34] or when Juno, trying to spirit Hannibal alive from the field of Zama, sends him a vision of Scipio that flees before him and leads him out of battle.[35] Because Vergil managed with great poetic effect to prolong Juno's wrath toward the refugees from Troy, toward Aeneas, the cousin of Paris, Silius Italicus thought he could revive her wrath toward the Romans of the sixth century. He did not care that peace had been made for some time, nor did he understand the passage in the *Aeneid* where Jove says to Juno, "Quae iam finis erit coniux? . . . Desine iam tandem. . . . Ulterius tentare veto," and after a brief exchange, "Annuit his Iuno, et mentem laetata retorsit."[36] This amounts to: the story is

---

[32] [Ed.] Silius Italicus (25–101) composed a long poem, *De bello punico*, which, in seventeen books, tells the events of Roman and Carthaginian history.

[33] Vergil *Eclogue* 4.15–16:
. . . divisque videbit
Permixtos heroas. . . .

[34] Silius *De bello punico* 4.457–80.

[35] Silius *De bello punico* 17.522.

[36] Vergil *Aeneid* 12.793, 800, 806, 841. ["How will it end now, my wife? . . . Give up now at last. . . . Any further attempts I now forbid. . . . Juno consented and rejoiced."]

over, times and events are coming in which the gods cannot be introduced except by force.

Even Silius Italicus was accused of being too faithful to history. But this common criticism ignores the difficulty of preserving form while changing subject matter and falsely assumes that the same things can be done with history as with fable.

Like the *Aeneid,* the *Thebaid* of Statius [37] and the *Argonautica* of Valerius Flaccus [38] took their subjects from the heroic age. But they lacked a striking, steady connection with the origin, growth, or traditions, with the fortunes of a real living society like Rome. Does that make a difference? Stories based on mythology and originally taken as truth could still give pleasure and enjoyment as a special species of the verisimilar, but not indefinitely. It may be that for those who have had the good fortune to escape polytheism, "the quality of the marvelous (assuming it deserves that name) that the Joves and Apollos and other gods bring to poetry is not only far from all verisimilitude, but cold, insipid, and ineffective." [39] It does not follow, however, that for a polytheistic people it must have been an inexhaustible fount of curiosity and pleasure. This complaint comes from one of them:

> Expectes eadem a summo minimoque poeta. [40]

Where then were the Latin poets to find subjects for the epic, when history could not be taken as mythology and when mythology without history had become no more than an old story? The plant was dead, after having borne its immortal flower.

Modern literature also provides an immortal poem, [41] but immortal in a completely different sense, both in subject and in form. Certainly, the same cannot be said of the *Furioso,* whose subject

[37] [Ed.] Statius (Publius Papirius Statius), 61–96. The *Thebaid* takes as its subject the expedition of the Seven Kings against Thebes and the war of Eteocles and Polynices.

[38] [Ed.] Valerius Flaccus, dead about 90 A.D. His unfinished poem the *Argonautica* derives in part from that of Apollonius of Rhodes.

[39] Tasso, *Dell'arte poetica e in particolare, sopra il poema eroico,* disc. I.

[40] Juvenal *Satires* 1.6. ["Expect the same commonplaces from the best and from the worst poets."]

[41] [Ed.] Manzoni refers here to Dante.

matter is earthly and historical. Still, it is well known that fictitious ideas about that era had been widely accepted for some time and had become common poetic material. Ariosto therefore did not have to face history; he had only to continue a fiction. The fiction might not prevail much longer, but it lasted long enough to elicit from him his first and only masterpiece.[42]

The first poem to bear the purpose and form of both the classical and historical epic was Trissino's *Italia liberata*.[43]

How this work could ever have won a reputation in its own time, or maintained it thereafter, would be a mystery, were it not for one particular fact, namely, the conviction that art could only find its true and unique perfection in the works of antiquity. This con-

---

[42] Why is it that of all the poems produced from this epic in its primitive state, "not one has remained a great monument of the literature to which it belonged, figuring in it as the *Iliad* or the *Odyssey* does in Greek literature, the *Ramayana* and the *Mahabharata* in that of India?" It is a question posed by Fauriel (*Histoire* 3:382), who also pinpoints the principal reason for the difference. "The *Iliad* and the *Ramayana*, he says, are not just popular poems; they are, or at least were, great national monuments, strictly historical, inasmuch as there was not a history which competed for their place; they were monuments consecrated by political and religious authority. Instead, the romantic epics, popular as they were in certain times and places, were never really national and never received the sanction of religion, science or art." In fact, except for a few incidental strokes of beauty that Fauriel attests can be found in some of these poems, they could not, on account of their origin, be such as to merit even the sanction of art. Composed for a single class of persons, the more ignorant class (because there were historical accounts of these facts, and people to read them), and composed to elicit belief, their material was necessarily geared, not to the general level of intellect, but to a particular one—the lowest. Error is always, basically, a miserable thing, notwithstanding all the appearance lent by external ornament, so I would not want to call the lies of the *Iliad* beautiful by any means. But it does not ever seem likely to me that an error that faced positive and known truths, or knowable ones, and that needed to find in minds a special ignorance in order to be believed could be capable of very convincing inventions. Nor does it seem to me that the minstrels who addressed that ignorance, and to such an end, could be minds capable of splendid inventions. It was the historical epic, with the sad addition of the design to deceive. It does not seem to me that its results can be the object of a living, enduring curiosity. Vico, with good reason, could call Homer "the first historian who ever came to us from all the gentiles" (*Discoverto del vero Omero*), because from what whole peoples could believe, one can infer what they are. From romantic poems of the Middle Ages, one can learn only what one could lead the ignorant masses to believe.

[43] [Ed.] Giangiorgio Trissino (1478–1550), Italian poet whose works include *Sofonisba* (1515), the first regular Italian tragedy, *Gli simillini* (1547), a comedy, and *L'Italia liberata dai goti* (1527–1548).

viction persisted into Trissino's time, even though by then Italian poetry had already made great strides along a path quite different from the one marked out by the Greek and Roman classics, and even though the great vernacular poets, as they were called, had become very popular. According to this view, the new poetry had as many blanks as the number of poetic genres handed down from antiquity. A growing study of Latin literature, the gradual unearthing of buried ruins, the rediscovery of the riches of Greek writing after the fall of Constantinople—all of these had heightened immeasurably the desire to see these voids filled. Trissino stepped forward stoutly to fill two of the more significant of them. He gave modern literature its first traditional tragedy—*Sofonisba*—and its first traditional epic poem—*L'Italia liberata*. And he would have been quick enough, had Ariosto not beaten him to it,[44] to also give modern literature, in his *Simillini,* its first traditional comedy in verse. You can be sure, however, that if it had been a chivalric epic that he had written with similar inventiveness, style, and versification, it surely would have failed to achieve even the passing popularity of the *Amadigi* of Bernardo Tasso,[45] the *Giron Cortese* of Luigi Alamanni,[46] and a few other such works; it would have gone unnoticed from the start. But *L'Italia liberata* professed to meet a need, almost to fulfill a duty, of the new poetry and for this reason earned the title of epic poem—a title it still keeps even if it is no longer read, much like certain princes, who retain titles to lost or pretended realms, even if they are no longer obeyed. That poem—for I have no other term for it—failed to move the long-dormant historical epic a single step forward or back. Only the fact that it came first has kept its empty reputation alive. Nothing more about it need be said.

One of history's few famous epic poems, Camoëns's *Os Lusiadas,*[47] which came to light about a half-century later, has survived

---

[44] [Ed.] The first regular comedy in Italian literature was the *Cassaria* of Ariosto, presented in Ferrara in 1508.

[45] [Ed.] The father of Torquato Tasso. He lived from 1493 to 1569; his poem, the *Amadigi,* was never very popular.

[46] [Ed.] Born in Florence in 1495, exiled to France, where he was welcomed by Francis I, then Henry II, Luigi Alamanni died in Amboise in 1556.

[47] [Ed.] Camoëns (1524–80), the greatest Portuguese poet. *Os Lusiadas* was published in 1572. The subject of it is the discovery of the Indies by Vasco da Gama.

for completely different reasons and with a completely different sort of reputation. This poem is doubly historical, so to speak, since it gives at least as much emphasis to the history of other times as to the history that is its main subject. The principal action of the poem is the expedition of Vasco da Gama, but its real subject is Portugal, much as that of the *Aeneid* was Rome. But neither Portuguese nor any other modern history can be fully evoked with a handful of allusions. One simply cannot cover it in its fullness by touching only on great and well-known events as Vergil did with Roman history. There was no better way for Camoëns to become a consistently and monumentally patriotic poet like Vergil—to the extent that was possible—than to bring the history of his country into his poem at great length. The history that precedes the action of the plot comes in by way of a tale told by Vasco da Gama to an African king; later history, by way of a prediction. This was history's new and singular way of intruding on the epic even when not called for by the main action of the plot. Yet why do I say "intruding," when history is only coming back home?

But, after all, I hear that I must move on to another man and another poem. Granted, I am told, this epic genre is no longer the spontaneous epic of Homer or the fictional epic of Vergil. Granted, it is the historical epic that Lucan founded, Silius Italicus reformed, and Trissino revived. Granted, its purpose is wholly foreign to the knowledge and spirit of our day. Still, it has given us the *Gerusalemme liberata*—a work that has for almost three centuries (and with only a few rather famous exceptions like Galileo,[48] but exceptions all the same) given pleasure and inspiration to the learned and cultivated not only of Italy but of all the world.

What of it? When I said before that the chivalric epic died, did I deny that the *Furioso* has lived on? Did Tasso, when he insisted that "the subject of the heroic poem be drawn from the history of not too remote an age,"[49] mean to remove the *Aeneid* from the

---

[48] [Ed.] Guise notes that this is an allusion to the *Considerazioni sul poema del Tasso* by Galileo (1590).

[49] Tasso, *Dell'arte poetica*, disc. 1. The drawback that Tasso finds in an ancient subject will certainly strike no reader as the principal or the real drawback. And one can see even here an indication of how much the demands of history have grown. "The history of the earliest times," says Tasso, "greatly helps the poet in imagining,

ranks of living poems because its subject came from the age of fables, a time very remote even for Vergil? Certainly not. Tasso was
not referring to what had already been done, but to what could be
done again. And, by the same token, I would not conclude from the
fact that the European public continued to praise the *Gerusalemme*
that it wanted the epic genre to continue being written. On the contrary, it would seem to mean that, after the *Gerusalemme,* the public wanted to call the writing of such poems to a halt.

You may be wondering where I find this injunction.

My answer is that there are two ways to forbid something, one
direct, the other indirect. An example of the latter is the extrava-
gant customs duties that discourage the purchase of dutiable goods
(contraband excepted!). Something similar may be going on here.
The epic poem became a superhuman work that, while not strictly
speaking impossible, cannot reasonably be expected to recur. It has
never been thought strange that numbers of people should write
other sorts of poetry or that someone should strive for a new genre,
even of a narrative kind. But it is hard to imagine someone setting
out to write an epic poem, an epic poem in the strict sense of the
word. To do so is almost like promising a miracle, an impossible
goal. The poet's own friends are dismayed, and they almost embrace him tearfully, as if he were setting off for unknown parts
across forbidding seas, on a more rugged and perilous exploit than
even those he intends to depict, as if, for all I know, he were setting
off for a battle with supernatural beings.

Certainly, like all extraordinary works, extraordinary poetry is

---

for when events are buried in the bosom of antiquity with scarcely a weak or obscure
memory remaining of them, the poet is free to change them and change them again,
and, without any respect at all for the truth, narrate them as he pleases. But with this
advantage comes a disadvantage, that together with ancient times one must introduce ancient customs. But the manner of making war and arming oneself, practiced
by the ancients, along with almost all their habits, cannot be read without an-
noyance by the majority of people today." The real reason, and what now comes
suddenly to mind, is that one can know something about antiquity and one can infer
something; and it is for this that antiquity interests us. As soon as it has become the
study of erudite philosophers, it can no longer be the material of poets. It is like a
manuscript worm-eaten here, faded there, but, by looking intently one can read
what remains and try to tell from it what is missing. The modern poetry upon antiquity would be like the scribblings of a child upon that manuscript or, better, like the
block letters that a more grown-up child would write upon it.

a rare and difficult thing. But unless one believes, as one surely cannot, that the difficulty of a poetic work is a function of its length, it is not at all clear why, of all outstanding poetry, the epic should be so singularly difficult.

"There is hardly any ordinary novel," said Voltaire, "in which events are not better laid out, more artistically arranged, or put together with vastly greater skill than in the poetry of Homer."[50] The claim may seem exaggerated, but I believe it is basically true, especially if we look at the great many novels produced since Voltaire was writing and, in particular, at the few that have remained famous. True, the structuring of events, the organization of lesser events around a principal one, and the achievement of overall unity are precisely what make the writing of epic poetry so difficult and almost miraculous, though other skills may also be critically important. But it is hard to see why anyone blessed with these gifts should not be able to use them as successfully in the epic poem as elsewhere. I am inclined to believe that the notion that the epic is so very difficult to produce arises from a certain confused awareness that the genre itself is intrinsically flawed. The epic poem is looked upon as so extraordinarily problematic because it seems to be like the squaring of a circle. One wonders how nature could possibly produce someone capable of representing a great event in epic form. This somewhat confused question really amounts to this: how can anyone properly represent a great event while misrepresenting it?

Just mentioning Voltaire should bring to mind (as if we needed reminding) the successful breach of this injunction by *La Henriade*, a work that had an almost universal appeal when it first appeared and has kept it to this day. But the *La Henriade* only illustrates all the better how the difficulty had increased by that time and to what lengths the poet had to go to overcome it. When I open *La Henriade*, I find, before reaching *La Henriade* itself, an "Idea of *La Henriade*" and a "Succinct History of Events on Which the Plot Is Based," and I find after it a long string of historical notes, and an "Essay on the Civil Wars in France."[51] Tasso quite rightly criticized

[50] Voltaire, *Essai sur la poésie épique*, chap. 2.
[51] [Ed.] The first two works cited by Manzoni are ordinarily presented in inverse order. The "long string of historical notes" follows the "Essay on the Civil

poets of his day for doing considerably less than that. He said of the *Iliad,* "Its plot is absolutely perfect and comprehensive. There is no need to look outside for help in understanding it. We complain about modern works when they make us resort to prose that they carry before them like a written declaration. Clarification that comes from discussions and other such devices is neither artistic nor characteristically poetic, but extrinsic and borrowed." [52]

Exactly, but the problem is to avoid needing such devices. Homer certainly did not have to resort to historical explanations or evidence, for he was writing history himself. Memory was his guarantor; all he had to do was invoke it at the outset and then occasionally throughout. Vergil did not need such devices either, in spite of the fact that his situation was very different. He related things that could not be believed; he was not writing history. But never mind, there was no history about his subject that he could cite or had to fear. Even in Tasso's time, there doubtless was much less need for such aids than in Voltaire's. The demand for factual truth from poets could not have been very strict or rigorous if it was so easily satisfied by historians and if poetry still figured so prominently within history itself. In fact, largely poetic stories about the origins of nations and states were still recited with confidence and willingly accepted. Even as to more recent events, just finding them verisimilar was generally enough to keep both writers and readers of history from inquiring whether they were sufficiently documented. Certain old objections notwithstanding, the dialogue that historians put in the mouths of their characters did not seem out of place, because at that time historians, much like poets, were turning these characters into fictional figures of their own.

None of this, I believe, requires proof. But let me cite a well-known example from a somewhat earlier period, though not so much earlier as to be considered, in this respect at least, a different era. Unless I am mistaken, even so thoughtful and sound an observer as Machiavelli—that is, when he is not using expediency as

---

Wars in France." It contains a "Dissertation on the Death of Henry IV," an "Extract on the Criminal Trial of Racaillac of May 19, 1610," and an "Extract of the Trial of the Question of May 27." (Noted by Guise, p. 473.)

[52] Tasso, *Dell'arte poetica,* disc. 2.

his ultimate standard of judgment and advice, a standard that is iniquitous, therefore absurd, and also quite useless for getting to the bottom of things—offers not a single example of historical criticism throughout his many and varied observations in the *Discourses on Titus Livy*. This is striking, for since Machiavelli insisted that his lessons be drawn from facts, the truth of those facts must have been not just important to him but absolutely essential. Yet, when Machiavelli chooses to cite passages, he takes his primary text as often from Livy's dialogue as from Livy's historical narrative. In fact, he even goes so far as to cite one passage where the historian, more the poet than ever, describes the inner workings of the soul. In his famous chapter on conspiracies,[53] speaking of "the dangers one encounters in an undertaking," Machiavelli says: "And how men's minds become seized and confounded, Titus Livy could not point out better than by saying the following words as he describes how Alexamenes the Aetolian discovered, when the time came to carry out his plan to kill Nabis the Spartan, that he had to tell his soldiers what to do: 'Collegit et ipse animum, confusum tantae cogitatione rei.'"[54]

I scarcely mean to suggest that Machiavelli took everything he found in Livy as positive truth. The very expression, "Titus Livy could not point out better," is one that Machiavelli could as easily have used if he had been referring to an apologue. With the same indifference, Machiavelli sometimes says, when quoting dialogue, "Their praetor Annius spoke these words," or, "Let me give you the words of Papirius Cursor"; but he sometimes says, "Our historian puts these words into his mouth," or "One can tell by the words which Livy has him say." It is precisely this indifference toward the positive reality of historical facts, this intellectual pursuit of whatever may be interesting even if it is only verisimilar, and stopping there, that I wanted to show in Machiavelli, as a famous example of a quite common attitude. But since this attitude was not based on reason, it could not go on indefinitely. By Voltaire's day, it had so

---

[53] [Ed.] Machiavelli, *Discorsi* 3:6.

[54] ["He summons his spirit to himself, confounded by reflections on such a great matter."]

diminished that he felt compelled as a lesser evil to place all those historical props under his poetic structure.[55]

I was going to add that even Tasso, at one point in his career, gave other evidence of feeling increasingly the inconvenient pressures of history, for he put far more history in the *Conquistata* than he had put in the *Liberata*.[56] But this argument would be controversial, and I would be accused of disrespect, of taking the aberration of a great man seriously. Rather than let myself become an accomplice of the foolish and irreverent critics who caused the tormented and maddened poet to sacrifice his genial inspirations, I shall leave my observations in the pen and go on saying to myself:

It could not have been the criticisms of others that led Tasso to give history a greater place in his second poem, for the criticism that was made of him on this point—inappropriately, of course, but that is beside the point—was, instead, "that the *Gerusalemme liberata* is mere history without fiction."[57] Bastiano de' Rossi, his chief opponent in the literary debate all too typical of Italy those days, objected, "A poet is not a poet without inventing; once he writes history, or writes about the history others have written, he loses his identity altogether."[58] The change in Tasso's work must have come about differently. I may be wrong, but I think it must have come about this way: when Tasso made his most unfortunate decision to rewrite his poem and reexamined the chronicles of the Crusades to see whether there was anything of his to touch up from a historical point of view, history probably had its natural effect, which is to seem more suitable than invention to a subject that is history and not invention. He was unable to tell history, "Go in peace, for you have played your part," because the part that history should play in the epic poem, or better, the part that invention should play in de-

[55] [Ed.] We recall that Manzoni felt the same need for historical props when he composed his tragedies. Both the *Adelchi* and the *Carmagnola* are accompanied by historical notes.

[56] [Ed.] The *Gerusalemme conquistata* (1593) is the result of the revision of the *Gerusalemme liberata*, which was composed in 1575 and published in 1581.

[57] *Discorso di Orazio Lombardelli intorno ai contrasti che si fanno sopra La Gerusalemme liberata*, in *Opere di Torquato Tasso* (Florence, 1724), 6:224.

[58] *Degli accademici della Crusca, difesa dell'Orlando Furioso contra 'l dialogo dell'epica poesia di C. Pellegrino*, in *Opere di Tasso* 5:406.

picting a historical event, had not been determined by Tasso's times or, for that matter, ever since. In his somewhat earlier *Discorso dell'arte poetica,* Tasso had laid down the rule: "Leave the beginning and the end of the enterprise, and some more famous things, historically intact, changed very little if at all. Change then, if you must, the means and circumstances; alter the time and sequence of other events; and prove yourself in all a more artful poet than a truthful historian." [59] I do not find it a bit surprising that Tasso later felt that "part of the most famous episode had been left out of the first" story of the *Gerusalemme,*[60] which had been created according to that rule. Who could ever expect to make the same judgment twice, even on one and the same question, when judging by such vague and nebulous criteria as "some more famous things," or "very little if at all," and such arbitrary and loose standards as "if you must," and being more poet than a historian. Nor do I find any more guidance when Tasso, by now unfortunately author of the *Conquistata,* says, "So far as the mixture of truth and falsehood is concerned, I believe that truth ought to have the greater role because there must be truth to the beginning of the plot, which is our entry into the whole, and to the end, where all events lead." [61] Positing "the greater role" is no more precise than saying "some more famous things," though I only see here confusion about the epic's purpose, not the derangement of a man.

I spoke earlier of *La Henriade* and of the fact that the author, by adding prose to it, now allowed history not only to occupy a greater place in the epic but to camp outside it as well. What does this prose contain? Accounts of prior and contemporaneous events that could not figure into the poem, but might be necessary to understand it fully; references to histories, memoirs, and letters, to alert the reader that a particular fact alluded to in the poem was actually true; appropriate commentary when the facts could be disputed; biographical sketches of one character or another to show that what the author has him say or do in the poem comports with what he knows of his personality and real behavior; and so on.

---

[59] Tasso, *Discorso,* pt. 2.

[60] *Giudizio sovra la Gerusalemme di Torquato Tasso, da lui medesimo riformata,* bk. 1, in *Opere* 4:132.

[61] Tasso, *Giudizio,* 132.

To be sure, Voltaire had here, as in almost all his writings in verse or prose, other aims too, or, rather, that constant and regrettable aim of attacking Christianity. There is no point in going into how he worked to this end through a subject in which the horrors committed under the pretext of Christianity gave him an even more specious pretext for condemning it and—to his and others' misfortune—an easier time making it seem hateful. But leaving aside the special use to which Voltaire was able to put these historical aids, was it idiosyncratic of him to resort to them? Hardly. It was only a product of having put so much history into the poem, which, in turn, was only a product of the changed conditions of the age, of readers no longer being able to see in history a simple means for creating something else. The author simply could not find a better means—and would you have been able to suggest one?—for conveying the special verisimilitude that tied his inventions to his subject.

What Horace suggested to a poet of his time—whether an epic or tragic poet is unimportant here—certainly was simpler, easier to do and, above all, more suitable to art: "Follow tradition." [62] But he could afford to suggest this because at the same time he proposed subjects such as Achilles, Medea, Ino, Ixion, Io, [63] Orestes—mytho-

---

[62] Horace *Ars poetica* 119–24:
Aut famam sequere aut sibi convenientia finge.
Scriptor, honoratum si forte reponis Achillem,
impiger, iracundus, inexorabilis, acer,
iura neget sibi nata, nihil non arroget armis.
Sit Medea ferox invictaque, flebilis Ino;
perfidus Ixion, Io vaga, tristis Orestes.
["Either follow tradition or, if you invent, see
that your invention is in harmony with itself.
If in your poem you are putting before us again
the honoring of Achilles, he must be spirited,
hot-tempered, ruthless, fiery, he must refuse
law as not made for him and claim the world as
the prize of arms. So Medea must be defiant
and untamed, Ino tearful, Ixion forsworn, Io
a wanderer, Orestes unhappy."]
[63] [Ed.] Ino: wife of Athamas, adventures told in Ovid *Metamorphoses* 4.416–562. Ixion had treacherously made his father-in-law fall into a burning furnace (see Vergil and Ovid). Io: see her role in Aeschylus's *Prometheus Bound* 561–886.

logical subjects—which means that they were well known and that, beyond the common knowledge surrounding them, there was absolutely nothing positive and verifiable to be known. There were, in fact, some people who did "know" more, but what was it they knew? A greater quantity of arbitrary and, therefore, diverse and discrepant inventions. Erudition in such matters was not, nor could it have been, anything but an accumulation of largely divergent and inconsistent things. For there was no rational basis for choosing among so many contradictory accounts, that is, no prevalence of authority—not just a real prevalence, but one palpable enough to gain general acceptance among the learned and to convince the public that, beyond what it knew, there was really something to know. Whatever little coherence and unity was to be found in that material came from common knowledge, from tradition, and this little bit was as subject to arbitrary additions as it was immune to factual ones. Thus, when the reader or spectator wanted to judge fairly and readily the verisimilitude of new poetic inventions, he had the other term of the comparison already set in his mind.[64] Under these circumstances, nothing could have been more appropriate than Horace's rule, or, rather—since in art, a rule can only serve to point the way—his suggestion. But how could this suggestion have served or satisfied Voltaire? How could tradition help him compose a *La Henriade* that would have a plot worthy of its subject matter and its time? The public doubtless knew something about Henry

[64] I said "judge" because that is the mind's procedure in such a case; and the fact that it is accompanied by emotions, even the liveliest, does not change its nature. They are those facile, ready, instantaneous judgments that develop and follow one another in the mind with indescribable rapidity, without attention being drawn by or reflection turning back upon any one of them. Those are judgments that, so to speak, serve the mind without occupying it and pass by in the process of having their effect, passing by either to become lost in forgetfulness or to hide in the base of the memory, where they lie unnoticed until some occasion arises to stir up one or more of them—an occasion that may never arise. How many such judgments, for instance, must an art critic have made in one moment without being able either to discern or relate them one moment later when, seeing a picture for the first time, he says suddenly, "It's by that artist." In fact, what else does one do if not induce from a multiple and rapid succession of judgments of special cases of the verisimilar when, upon hearing a word, a fact, an event about a known person or thing, one believes or disbelieves? And everyone knows that those judgments can sometimes be accompanied by more intense and profound emotions than those that art can ever excite.

IV, Catherine de' Medici, the League, and the siege of Paris. But it also knew that there was much more to be known, and, like it or not, the public would expect to be given additional information whenever and however the subject might arise. Anyone who tried to weave a poetic fabric of verisimilars on the thin and meager warp of common knowledge about that network of events would have sorely disappointed that expectation. The work would have seemed and would have been—in this respect only, of course—a continuation of the epic written by Jean Chapelain, Pierre La Moyne (le Père), Jean Desmarets, and Mme de Scudéry.[65] So here then is the poet himself reduced to supplying the reader with the necessary material for comparison, with a basis for judging the verisimilitude of his inventions. And since this could not be done within the confines of the poem itself, he is reduced to going outside it and making assertions, tests, arguments through what he more than once had called *vile prose.*

La Henriade also provides an occasion to observe another great problem of the historical epic, namely the supernatural "marvelous."

Whether or not the epic poem should contain elements of the marvelous is a question that has been resolved on several occasions, but in opposite ways.

I wonder whether those poets and critics who believed that the most important, if not all, the rules of art had to be found in Aristotle's *Poetics* noticed that the master is absolutely silent on a point so important to them. His silence must have struck them as strange, but it would seem quite natural to anyone who considers that the question had not yet arisen, and perhaps could not even have been foreseen, at the time Aristotle was writing. Aristotle speaks of the Homeric epic, the epic known and practiced in his own day. This was an epic that drew its subjects from the heroic age, subjects in which the supernatural was innate. For Aristotle, then, the marvelous, the supernatural, was implicit. The question, which never seems to get resolved, only originated when the epic began taking for its subjects events from historic times.

[65] Authors of *La Pucelle,* of *La Louisiade, Clovis,* and *Alaric:* poems that have remained celebrated by name, in part because they had been so once, in part because they were scorned by a poet of altogether different fame.

Some would argue that without the marvelous a poem can only be either a versified history or a history changed for no good reason. (After all, what justification can there be for altering the causes, the natural and true circumstances of an event, and substituting others that might be equally plausible, but are false?) Others contend that in the course of known or knowable events, fictitious miracles inevitably seem out of place, as indeed they are. Both are valid objections, I admit, but better for hindering than helping our resolution of the problem. In the end, the historical epic can say no more to the marvelous than what Martial said to the man with an uneven disposition: "I can neither live with you, nor without you."[66]

After eighteen centuries, the question is at the same crossroads where it found itself in its first steps: either eliminate the marvelous, like Lucan, or accept it perforce, like Silius Italicus. But—and this is a point that bears repeating—anyone who was a poet could, by following either path, accidentally establish his worth. This must have been the case with Voltaire, who introduced the marvelous into his poem, or rather two types of it, the Christian and the allegorical. But I am probably not alone in saying that, although these figures are embellished with vital and decorous imagery and with noble and august sayings—when they are just—and although the whole is dressed in verses that are nearly always beautiful, often exquisite, the two types of marvelous still give the action a weak and labored effect, acting in it almost like indifferent strangers who have to be sent for anew each time one wants them to appear.

Voltaire, it seems to me, contradicted himself when, as a poet, he used the marvelous and then, as a critic, insisted that one could do without it, although it is not at all unusual, when there are two plausible positions that may be taken, instead of a fixed rule, for the same person first to prefer one and then the other. "Vergil and Homer," he says, "did very well putting the gods on stage. Lucan did equally well without them. Jove, Juno, Mars, and Venus were necessary ornaments for the actions of Aeneas and Agamemnon. Little was known about those fabulous heroes. . . . But Caesar, Pompey, Cato, and Labienus lived in very different times than Aeneas."

[66] "Nec tecum possum vivere, nec sine te." Martial, "In habentem varios mores" (bk. 12, epigram 40).

And Henry IV, Mayenne, Potier, and Mornay?[67]

"The civil wars of Rome," he adds, "were too serious for such games of the imagination."

And the civil wars of France?

Can Voltaire apply these words to the mythological deities without applying them to the Christian supernatural? My answer is that, where the supernatural is invented by the poet rather than revealed, they apply just the same.

More interesting, in another respect, is what Voltaire says somewhat later:

> Those who confuse the origins of an art with its principles are convinced that a poem cannot exist without the gods, for the *Iliad* is filled with them. But these deities are so inconsequential to the epic that the most beautiful passage of the *Pharsalia,* or perhaps of any poem, is the discourse in which Cato, that stoic hater of fables, scornfully refuses to visit the temple of Jupiter.[68]

The implication of this statement should be obvious to all: if exquisite words can be uttered in contempt of polytheism, the epic surely can exist without the marvelous. But what bears special emphasis is that for Voltaire the historical epic was not simply a continuation, as commonly believed, but an evolution of the primitive, essentially mythic epic. It is as if the epic that purported to be history, and was accepted as such, was the same art as the epic that counterfeited history, without managing or even seeking to be believed, simply because the second imitated some extrinsic forms of the first. No, a genre that, having begun without principles, discovers them later through changes in purpose and effect, would be a new genre, even though it retains some of the old extrinsic forms. And what comes after is not always progress.

There is another type of epic that at first would seem to accommodate the supernatural, namely, those epics that draw their subjects from sacred history. But this very fact should make it clear that

---

[67] [Ed.] Charles de Lorena, duke of Mayenne; Louis Potier de Gesvres; and Philippe de Mornay Duplessis were French politicians and characters out of Voltaire's *La Henriade.*

[68] Voltaire, *Essai sur la poésie épique,* chap. 4.

this type too is prone, although in a different way, to the same drawback as the others. They are revisions of a history that is history in its strictest, most imposing sense. Here, the supernatural does not intrude upon the subject; invention intrudes upon the supernatural. I dare say that a respectful, highly rational intuition suggests that no human mind will ever find a rule of verisimilitude in the extraordinary displays of divine will and power, in the way that it finds one in the natural course of events or decisions of the human will. The magnificent passages found in *Paradise Lost*,[69] and the poetic talent that they almost inevitably reflect, still can only produce the effect of a constant interpolation. And even the *Messiah*[70] has some extraordinary merits, particularly that frequent union of the tender and sublime which produces a gentle and all the more pleasurable emotion. But its subject is as inexhaustibly suggestive as it is resistant to poetic embellishments.

This concludes my brief observations on the epic. There will be even less to say about the tragedy, to which I now turn. Please understand that I am dealing only with historical tragedy and only to the extent that it is historical.

The problems that history poses for this genre differ both in nature and degree from those of the epic, thanks to the essential difference in form of the two genres. Tragedy does not use the same vehicle for both history and invention, as the epic does in using narrative. The only immediate subject for the language of tragedy is the verisimilar; thus the discourses that Shakespeare, Corneille, Voltaire, and Vittorio Alfieri put into the mouth of Caesar are all poetic fabrications. On the other hand, Lucan relates actions of Caesar that can be either invented or real. In the epic, then, words may produce a poetic effect at one moment, a historical effect at the next—or, by failing to produce either, may remain ambiguous. In

[69] [Ed.] *Paradise Lost* of Milton, 1667.

[70] [Ed.] The *Messiah*, a religious epic by Friedrich Gottlieb Klopstock (published several times between 1748 and 1773). The idea of this work was suggested by Milton's poem. Milton had described man's fall; Klopstock resolved to write of the Redemption. Mme de Staël praises Klopstock for having "given the simplicity of the Gospel a poetic charm that does not alter its purity." Manzoni, with reason perhaps, did not share this opinion (Cited by Guise, 475).

tragedy it is only poetry that speaks; history effectively stands outside, related to the work but not a part of it.[71]

In tragedy, staging heightens greatly the impact of speech by
adding people and action to it. It is relevant—but also worth point-
ing out in its own right—that, due to their realistic appearance,
these sensory elements, far from impairing the effect of pure verisimilitude sought by art, actually support and strengthen it. The
reason is that these realities act simply as vehicles for verisimilar
action and are understood as such by the spectator. In fact, if an
actor were to do or say something in the middle of the play that
referred to his real-life personality or to real-life circumstances, it
would disturb the spectator by distracting him with that reality.
And what does this sensitivity suggest, if not that these realities had
deliberately been left out of consideration? So it is that the more
naturally an actor appears to act, and the more moving he is, the
more he focuses attention on the merely verisimilar; and the more
the actor personifies the character he is playing—the person struck
by misfortune, blinded by passion, or unaware of impending danger—the more he reduces and even effaces his real personality. This
is the highest praise an actor can earn and what was meant by

[71] To forestall a small objection, I ought to observe that in some tragedies, historical words are put into the mouth of one character or another; as, for instance,
the "Tu quoque, Brute?" of Caesar. But it is a rare drawback and, for the most part,
an avoidable one. I say drawback because the effect of such words is to divert the
mind from the mere verisimilar to the real. And I know well that to others this ability
to have a character say what an actual man said can seem an advantage, an occasion
not to miss. But I do not see how one can find in poetry an effective and powerful art
and at the same time find that it derives its power from something that produces an
effect opposite to its own.

The drawback thus would not be avoidable in the case cited and in several others, that is, when the historical words are famous, because by omitting them the poet
would not have prevented his spectator from remembering them; and the real Caesar
of history would, inevitably, insert himself in the spectator's mind, right in front of
the fictitious Caesar of the poet, like Sosia of Plautus in front of Mercury. But in the
cases of which we speak, it is the mortal that wins out. "Praefulgebant eo ipso quod
non visebantùr." And what does this mean? That history may want to enter the field
most exclusively proper to poetry when poetry gets historical. History records many
deeds, and many more than words, and thus it is much easier to avoid history when
making historical characters speak than when making them act. But these few words
have the same right as facts to want their place, and the same power to take it.

saying, for example, that Garrick was Hamlet, or Lekain was Orosmane.[72] It is not the reality of the stage—present, to be sure, but subordinate to the verisimilar—that can disturb this effect. What can disturb it is historical reality, which is independent of the verisimilar and upon which the verisimilar itself should depend, which may be known or simply knowable, and which, though absent from the senses, permeates the subject.

All of tragedy's advantages—the primary one of its dialogue form, the secondary but important one of staging, and still more subordinate ones not worth going into here—allow the tragedy, more easily than the epic, to shield itself from history.

I have said "shield itself," but I should add, "while still surrendering something," since even from the outside, history succeeds in making itself felt and its demands heard. The extrinsic but essential relationship that historical tragedy bears to history, and the resulting need to find verisimilar forms for historical subjects, had to produce—and did produce—the same problems for tragedy as for the epic. They may be less frequent and less obvious, but they grow all the same with the passage of time. Nothing makes this clearer than the lengths to which a great tragedian had to go to argue them away:

"The question," says Pierre Corneille, "whether changes may permissibly be made in subjects drawn from history or fable, seems to have been decided by Aristotle in rather formal terms. According to him, 'The traditional subjects should not be changed, Clytemnestra should be killed by Orestes, and Eriphyle by Alcmene.' This rule does, however, allow for certain distinctions and qualifications. The circumstances or, if you prefer, the means of leading up to the main action, surely remain in our control, for history often either does not provide them or provides so little of them that something else is necessary in order to complete the work. One could even safely presume that a spectator who has read about these circumstances beforehand will not remember them clearly enough to no-

---

[72] [Ed.] David Garrick (1717–79), the most celebrated English actor, who excelled in Shakespearean roles, especially Hamlet. Henri-Louis Lekain (1728–78), renowned French actor, interpreter of Voltaire. His greatest triumph was the role of Orosmane in *Zaïre*.

tice the changes and accuse us of lying, as he doubtless would if he caught us changing the main action."[73]

Thus, while classical tragedy proceeded on an assumption of knowledge by the spectator, modern tragedy is reduced to relying on forgetfulness! An unfortunate premise, since in art the fear of knowledge is not a healthy sign. It is also a precarious one, for if the spectator who had forgotten the historical circumstances of the subject and could thoroughly enjoy the poetic fiction at the first performance leaves the theatre with renewed interest in the subject and repairs to the book where he had first read of those circumstances to refresh his memory, the second performance is unlikely to find him as conveniently forgetful as before. Finally, it is a premise about which Corneille contradicts himself, since if the circumstances remain in the poet's control, it should make no difference whether the spectator does or does not remember those of history. In the *Analysis* which he added to his works, Corneille discusses more than once the changes he has made in history. In justifying these changes, indeed, openly accusing himself of them, Corneille reveals them and thus removes from under the historical tragedy that poor crutch of ignorance he had given it. To give such crutches to art is to admit that it has become crippled, and for a Pierre Corneille to give them to tragedy is a dire warning that there may no longer be a way to get it back on its feet.

But why did he need to make distinctions or qualifications in such a simple and adequate rule? Because the rule concerned one thing, and Corneille, following an already prevailing custom, had extended it to something else and something very different. Aristotle speaks of "accepted fables" and says they should not be changed;[74] Corneille speaks of subjects drawn either *from history*

---

[73] Pierre Corneille, *Second discours sur l'art dramatique.*

[74] "Acceptas quidem igitur fabulas (mythous) solvere non licet. Dico autem, seu Clytaemnestram necatam ab Oreste, et Eriphylen ab Alcmaeone." ["Hence, the Plot is the imitation of the action:—for by Plot I here mean the arrangement of the incidents" (Aristotle *Poetics* [trans. Butcher] 6.6).]

The word *mythos* came also to signify the particular form given to the action by each poet; and in this sense Aristotle uses it also, even defines it this way: "Est autem actionis quidem imitatio fabula: appello enim fabulam hanc compositionem rerum." ["He may not indeed destroy the framework of the received legends—the

or from fable, as if they were one and the same thing. Now the rule needed neither special qualifications nor distinctions when applied to "accepted fables" since they neither provided nor burdened the poet with anything but the principal action: Clytemnestra killed by Orestes, Eriphyle by Alcmene. The means and circumstances were fully in the poets' control. On the other hand, history provides, along with subjects, also means and circumstances that might not lend themselves so well to the purposes of art, hence the need to change them, or, rather, to alter the subjects with which they are, so to speak, associated. True, if history does not provide them, it leaves something to be desired; but that does not mean that poetic invention can supply them.

"The example of Clytemnestra's death," adds Corneille, "serves to prove my point. Both Sophocles and Euripides treated the subject, but with a different complication and a different denouement; and these differences distinguish the dramas, even though there is but one subject whose main action each of the poets retained."

And to do this, did they really need to qualify the rule? Not in the least. They obeyed it scrupulously, both of them having Clytemnestra die by Orestes' hand, and that being all the rule required. Or, rather, they anticipated a rule dictated by the practical needs of art, even before Aristotle had promulgated it. This privilege of every poet to invent freely a complication and a denouement of his own came about because they had nothing to go by but other plots and other denouements. There were poets against poets; verisimilars against verisimilars, tied to nothing but actions and characters as productive of invention as they were barren of binding historical circumstances. Inventing new circumstances was not a license that poets had to grab; it was the procedure proper to poetry. Aristotle himself acknowledges the need to invent when he hastens to add:

---

fact, for instance, that Clytemnestra was slain by Orestes and Eriphyle by Alcmaeon" (ibid., 15.5).] In the passage cited above, however, he cannot mean anything other than myths, in the proper and original sense of the word. In fact, how could one suppose that Aristotle advised the poet to follow the many and diverse compositions of other poets? Such an interpretation is contrary both to the idea itself and to the examples chosen by Aristotle, which are not examples of compositions, but of simple mythological themes, just as it is antithetical to the rest of the text that will be cited soon.

"It is then up to the poet to invent, and to make good use of the accepted fables."[75] Thus Corneille carves out as an exception to the rule what Aristotle considers its natural corollary. This is substantially the same rule that Horace later expressed with the words "famam sequere."[76]

What is more, neither Corneille's qualifications nor his consis-

[75] "Ipsum autem invenire oportet, et traditis uti recte" (Aristotle *Poetics*, chap. 4).

[76] [Ed.] Horace *Ars poetica* 119.

Another possible objection, and one not to hide. Even ancient Greek theater had historical tragedies, and from the outset—for example, the *Persiani* of Aeschylus. I will not ask here whether this work can be regarded as a tragedy; since one could ask the same question about other works by the same author, the subjects of which are taken from heroic times. But I will say that Greek tragedy did not continue along that path. The tragedies of Sophocles and of Euripides and the many among them of which Aristotle speaks in the *Poetics* are all composed upon mythological subjects. If the Greek theater had become historical, one would naturally have found it in the same straits as the modern theater; and Aristotle would have been hard pressed to find rules for it, if he had wanted to.

The Latin theater also had historical tragedies, and with Roman subjects, that were therefore called *praetexta;* and it had them, if not at the outset, that is from Livius Andronicus, Naevius, or Ennius, certainly not much later, since among the tragedies of Pacuvius, of which we have but titles and fragments, there is a *Paolus* (Emilius), and among those of Accius, a *Brutus* and a *Decius*. Horace praises this kind of tragedy in general, as an attempt at literary independence (*Ars poetica* 285–89):

> Nil intemptatum nostri liquere poetae;
> nec minimum meruere decus vestigia Graeca
> ausi deserere, et celebrare domestica facta,
> vel qui praetextas, vel qui docuere togatas.
> ["Our own poets have left no style untried,
> nor has the glory they have gained been
> least when they ventured to leave the
> footsteps of the Greeks and sing of native
> subjects, whether they have staged Roman
> tragedies or Roman comedies."]

But the fact that he does not lay down any precept for this kind of composition and merely points it out is reason to believe that it was not much cultivated; similarly, his constant return to poetry with Greek subjects is an indication that this was prevalent among many. And another indication of former times is that from Pacuvius there is but one historical tragedy; and from Accius two, against more than fifty with Greek subjects. Quintilian, in that brief summary he gives of the principal kinds of poetry and of the principal poets (*Institutes* 10.1) does not even make mention of *praetextae*. None had remained to us, and it is a misfortune: literary, to be sure. And one cannot get an idea of it from the *Octavia* of Seneca or from any Seneca play at all, these being the work of completely other times and of a completely different taste.

tently outstanding works could spare tragedy its ceaseless variations or give it a firm and definitive status in relation to history.

Fortunately for us, patient reader, there is no need to go over all these variations, even in haste, as we did with the epic. It should be enough here to describe the present state of affairs and its proximate causes. I would like to mention only one external variation in the intervening period which, though it did not go to the core of tragedy, was nonetheless very significant. Shortly after the middle of the last century, a French actor or actress (I do not know which) introduced a general reform in costuming to make it conform to the time in which the dramatic action was set. Before, it had partly reflected current fashion, partly the whims of the actors, partly customs of similar origin; there could also have been some sort of characteristic emblem drawn from history. Voltaire, I do not remember where, describes an actor in the age of Louis XIV who was playing Augustus in *Cinna*,[77] wearing a great wig and on top of this a large hat with long feathers decked with laurel leaves; the rest was in the same taste. And what does all this suggest? That the spectators were more disposed than in later times to see in the actor the poet's Augustus, the verisimilar Augustus, without giving very much thought to the real Augustus of history. The introduction of history even into the wings of the stage to control the actors, the born ministers of poetry, and to force them to wear its uniforms, was a sign of history's growing possession of tragedy and an indication of the greater possession it sought.

In fact, history did not have to wait long before initiating the revolution in drama that we now see triumphant. There was then a virtual consensus among the learned and cultured of Europe that the veritable tragedy, that which could satisfy "good taste" and be accepted by "good sense," was the tragedy in which the so-called unities of time and place were maintained, unities said to have been proclaimed by Aristotle, faithfully observed in Greek tragedy, and above all demanded by reason. Whether Aristotle actually proposed these unities, whether they had truly been observed in Greek tragedy, whether reason really had nothing to say against them,

---

[77] [Ed.] *Cinna*, a tragedy by Pierre Corneille.

hardly anyone asked; and whoever did was taken to task.[78] It is perfectly obvious that those rules did not suit history in the least. And the attempts that history had made up to that time, and continued to make, to assume a greater role in tragedy did in fact achieve something: tragedy, even at the cost of crippling itself, did all it

[78] If only they had attributed them to anyone else! But to imagine that Aristotle, who teaches so openly and repeatedly that the universal, the verisimilar, is the material proper to poetry, opposing it to history, whose material is the particular, the real, could take as the measure and the criterion of the verisimilar the material reality of the performance, the real circumstances of the spectator! It was like making a master of perspective say that a view, in order to be verisimilar, ought to represent only the objects that could actually stand within the limits of the frame. And because he says (*Poetics* chap. 2) that "tragedy strives to restrict itself to one cycle of the sun, or to vary little from it" (a practice that accorded well with the nature of mythological subjects), to believe that he meant with this formally to establish a limit to the ideal time of the action! He who, in the very *Poetics* where he treats the length of the fable expressly protests that such a limit cannot be established a priori! After having said that the material length of the drama is not something that concerns art, and turning to ideal duration, he says: "As far as the nature of the thing is concerned, the greater duration is the more beautiful, as long as it is not such as to make one lose a clear sense of the whole. In a word, the proper duration will be whatever is required so that, with the development of events according to the verisimilar or the necessary, one passes from unhappiness to happiness or vice versa." ("Terminus autem rei ex ipsius natura, semper quidem qui maior est, dummodo maneat intra eos fines ut una totus perspicuus sit, pulchior est. Ut autem simpliciter, re definita, dicamus, in quanta magnitudine, secundum verisimile, vel necessarium, deinceps nascentibus rebus, contingit in res secundas ex adversis, vel ex rebus secondis in adversas mutari, idoneus terminus est magnitudinis.") (Chap. 5.)

And since it is always helpful to know the origin of errors that have been much in fashion, in whatever matter, I thus add that the author of the rule of the two famous unities was, it would appear, Lodovico Castelvetro. At the beginning of those passages cited here, this critic, in his famous commentary on the *Poetics* of Aristotle, not only takes the mention of a particular fact for a general rule but adds to it something of his own that was needed to make it a rule, that is, a rationale. And it is that very antipoetic, antiphilosophical, and anti-Aristotelian rationale of verisimilitude relative to the performance and the spectator: a rationale that was then always alleged as the fundamental principle behind the rule. Moreover, Castelvetro criticizes Aristotle for not having applied it rigorously because Aristotle did not know it well: which is true enough. And upon that rationale he founds yet another unity, that of place, which one could never in any way have extracted from the *Poetics* of Aristotle. I translate Castelvetro's words here, in their original crudeness, begging the reader pardon for it. "The epic, narrating with words alone, can recount an action accomplished in many years and in different places without any disadvantage, the words presenting to our mind the expanses of time and place. This the tragedy cannot do, for it must rather have as a subject an action happening in a small bit of

could to accommodate history, short of infringing the rules. There was talk, it is true, of a certain Shakespeare who, either by ignoring them or simply not knowing them, managed to create something of value. But one spoke of him as of a savage genius, an eccentric brain with some remarkable lucid intervals, a kind of arid and steep mountain where a botanist, after climbing the bare rocks, might find some rare flowers. Furthermore, what was quoted from that great and unique poet came from those dramas of his in which history had the least part or no part at all. But look, in Germany another such poet is coming forward named Goethe who, in taking the path of the historical drama marked out by the "savage genius," and in taking it—as happens with great talents—without intention or fear of imitating, from his first steps forward imposes the rationale of history on his nation at the expense of the two unities. But in France, long proud of poets who had taken the other path, and in Italy, also proud of a recent poet, it was a different story. "What!" they said. "The rules to which a Corneille, a Racine, a Voltaire, an

---

space and a small interval of time, that is, in that place and that time where and when the performer remains occupied by the performance, and not in other places, nor in other times. But since the narrow space is the stage, thus the narrow time is what the spectators can at their ease experience while seated in the theatre, which I do not see exceeding the cycle of the sun, as Aristotle says, that is, twelve hours. This is because the bodily needs prevent people from continuing beyond the prescribed limit of their stay in the theatre: eating, drinking, relieving the superfluous weight of belly and bladder, sleep, and other necessities. Nor is it possible to lead them to believe that several days and nights have passed, when they know that only a few hours have passed, deception having no place for them since the senses always detect it." (*Poetica d'Aristotle,* trans. and set forth by Lodovico Castelvetro [Basel, 1576], 109.)

Then in the comment to the second passage, he rejects the rationale given by Aristotle for the particular, special, and relative duration of various plots; and he draws the attention of his source to that great rationale of probability relative to the performance and to the spectator. I quote here too: "Aristotle saw that the plots of tragedy usually ended at the end of the change, and that the things that happened and were contained in the fable did not extend beyond the limit of one cycle of the sun through the hemisphere, that is, beyond twelve hours; and not recognizing the true rationale for such a limit of actions gathered into a fable, he imagined that it was because of the capacity and nature of the listeners' memories, as if they would forget the first parts of the story if it contained an action of many days by the time they heard and saw the last parts. . . . So brief a limit was not imposed because of a weakness of memory, but for the reason we have already assigned: the representation itself and the comfort of the spectators, the representation taking as much time

Alfieri submitted—not to mention the authors of the *Merope* and the *Aristodemus*[79]—now seem a burdensome constraint on genius, an obstacle to perfection! How the proving grounds must have narrowed!" I do not know whether proposing that those rules be abolished seemed more an intolerable temerity or a wretched folly. But, for history to burst into tragedy as it intended, it actually had to knock down that bulwark, and it did. This is clearly the case in France; and even in Italy, as far as I can tell, the spectator neither suffers nor resents it if, in the course of a tragedy, he sees one scene end and another begin and if, in those three or four hours of sitting, the poet claims to show him more than that blessed circuit of the sun mentioned so innocently by Aristotle.

And so we see how what has been repressed becomes coercive itself once it is finally set free. Until then, the least particularized subjects of history had seemed most appropriate for tragedy, since they left most room for invention. If history is silent, said the poet, so much the better: I will speak. Now, on the contrary, it is the

---

as the real action would take and the people being unable to stay in the theater without intolerable discomfort for more than twelve hours." (Pp. 170, 171). And Castelvetro was reproached with being too subtle! But clever he certainly was, since the argument he brought up and left prevailing in the literary world could make not only critics but poets—and among them some great poets—lose sight, in this particular, for several generations, that poetry is poetry, that it is an art, and that, consequently, the means that one suggests to help it function either are not suitable and must be refuted or they are suitable, which means that one can abstract from whatever is heterogeneous to the purposes of art. To admit that a tragedy (verisimilar action) can be represented is to admit that the actual reality of things that make the representation possible cannot and must not count any more than the real quality of metallic green counts in the green of a painted tree. To say that tragedy becomes false if the representation does not agree with the real circumstances of the spectator is to say that a painting representing a snowfall becomes false for whoever looks at it in the month of July. It is not a question—either in painting or in poetry—of leading someone to believe (a silly phrase in such a subject), but of representing verisimilars, that is, ideal truths.

In so far as those rules were supposed to be faithfully observed in Greek tragedies, Corneille in the *Discourses* cited above adduced several proofs to the contrary; and many more Pietro Metastasio then adduces in his *Observations* upon all of these tragedies; but with all that, that those two rules had been observed in Greek tragedies was for a long time *the fact.*

[79] [Ed.] Manzoni thinks here of Scipio Maffei (1675–1755), author of a *Merope* that was presented in Modena in 1713, a very successful and often translated piece, and of Vincenzo Monti (1754–1828), author of the *Aristodemos.*

poets who, when the history books lack details, search them out in any available kind of document to amplify or even locate their subject. They are very happy if they manage to produce a more complete idea of the historical fact they are depicting, and even happier if they come up with a new idea, different from the one commonly held.[80] This is exactly the opposite of *famam sequere,* but how could it be otherwise? It is simply too contradictory to demand that poetry, to be effective, not lag behind the knowledge of its day, that it reflect and even anticipate reasonable intellectual trends, and at the same time demand that poetry, to remain as free as possible, not burden itself with such things.

Now that the facts are out, only a few questions remain:

Does anyone think tragedy could return to its old borders and keep its secrets with history, as it did for so long? Does anyone else believe that, with the expansion of tragedy's borders, we have finally found the proper measure of history's part in tragedy and the right way to mix it with invention? And if no one believes that, is there any reason to believe that this measure and this way will be found in the future?

You, reader, may reach your own conclusions.

Coming, finally, to the comparison between the purpose of the epic and tragedy, on the one hand, and the purpose of the historical novel, on the other, it is easy to see that the essential difference is this: that the historical novel does not draw its principal subject from history in order to transform it with poetic intent, but invents it, like the work from which it has taken its name and of which it is a new form. I mean the novel in which contemporary actions are invented: a completely poetic work, since within it both deeds and words are all merely verisimilar. But it is poetic, let us understand, in the sense of that lowly poetry that can grow out of the verisimilar of private modern actions and habits, and that takes the form of prose. With these words I certainly do not mean to align myself with those who mourn, or used to mourn—since it should have ended by now—those poetic pagan ages, those beautiful illusions

---

[80] [Ed.] This is the attitude of Manzoni himself, concerning historical tragedies. The *Discorso sopra alcuni punti della storia longobardica in Italia* was, we remember, the result of research to which he dedicated himself in order to write the *Adelchi.*

lost forever.[81] What differentiates us from people of those times is the possession of a historical criticism that seeks the real truth in past facts and, what is so much more important, the possession of a religion which, being the truth, cannot conveniently be adapted to arbitrary changes and fanciful elaboration. Is this something to complain about?

To return to their essential difference, the historical novel does not suffer, as do the epic and the tragedy—and the respect we owe to the famous souls who labored to create these forms should not keep us from criticizing the forms themselves—from that coarse fiction that consists of packing a true, celebrated, and therefore necessarily important event with fables. The principal subject of the historical novel is completely the author's, completely poetic, because merely verisimilar. Both the purpose and design of the author are, as much as possible, to make the subject and all the action so verisimilar with respect to the time in which they are set that they would have seemed probable even to people of that time, had the novel been written for them.

But—and here is the problem common to the historical novel and all types of poetry that invent things about the past—it is written for others. Let us imagine that an author has succeeded in composing a story which would have seemed verisimilar to people of that time. This effect would depend on a spontaneous and immediate comparison between the general notions conceived by the author and the real ones that the readers arrive at through experience. On the other hand, to produce this effect in people of another time, the author must try to compensate for experience with information and, as it were, try to put the original and the portrait into a single work. Thus there is not the direct contrast between the true and the verisimilar, and this is doubtless a great advantage, but at the same time there is either a confusion of the two or a division between them. In fact, as was demonstrated perhaps at greater length than necessary in the first part of this essay, there are inevitably, in widely varying proportions, both confusion and division.

---

[81] [Ed.] Among those one can cite, for instance, Vincenzo Monti (*Su la mitologia*), Giacomo Leopardi (*Alla primavera*), and Friedrich Schiller (*Ode to the Gods of Greece, Letters on the Aesthetic Education of Man*).

But it is no wonder that while the conviction still lasted that history and invention could go well together, it occurred to a man of exceptional talent to combine them in a new and more plausible fashion that accommodated a far greater quality and variety of historical material. And it is even less a wonder that, implemented by such an imaginative, observant, fertile, and discerning talent, it could produce an extraordinary effect on the public of all cultured nations, an effect with which we are all familiar.

But will that advantage at least be enough to assure the historical novel a long life?

This is no happy question for one who loves the historical novel. When things are misused, the remedy sometimes yields to the abuse; and there is no less congenial place for error, no place where it is less able to hold its own than beside truth. It is undeniable that what first won favor for the historical novel was precisely the illusion of history, and it may be that that illusion will not last long. How many times has it been said, and even written, that the novels of Walter Scott were truer than history! But those are the sort of words that get by in the first blush of enthusiasm and are not repeated upon reflection. For if by history is meant any book that claims that title, the remark amounts to nothing; and if by history is meant all facts and customs that could possibly be known, it is plainly false. To convince oneself of this at once—though these are not things that get settled at once—just ask whether the idea of the various novels of Walter Scott was more truthful than the idea on which he had based them. It was, in fact, an idea more vast, but at the price of being less historical. Another truth had been added, but of a different nature, and therefore the idea as a whole was no longer true. A great poet and a great historian may be found in the same man without creating confusion, but not in the same work. In fact, the two opposite criticisms that furnished the lines of argument for the trial of the historical novel had already showed up in the first moments of the genre and at the height of its popularity, like germs of an eventually mortal illness in a healthy-looking baby.

And is the historical novel still popular? Is there the same desire to write historical novels and the same desire to read those that are already written? I don't know, but I can not help imagining that, if this essay had come out some thirty years ago, when the world was eagerly awaiting and avidly devouring the novels of Walter Scott, it would have seemed eccentric and brash in its treatment of the historical novel. Nor can I help imagining that, if anyone now were willing to trouble himself enough to call it these names, it would be for an altogether different reason. And thirty years ought to be no time at all for a genre of art that was destined to live on.

INDEX

130